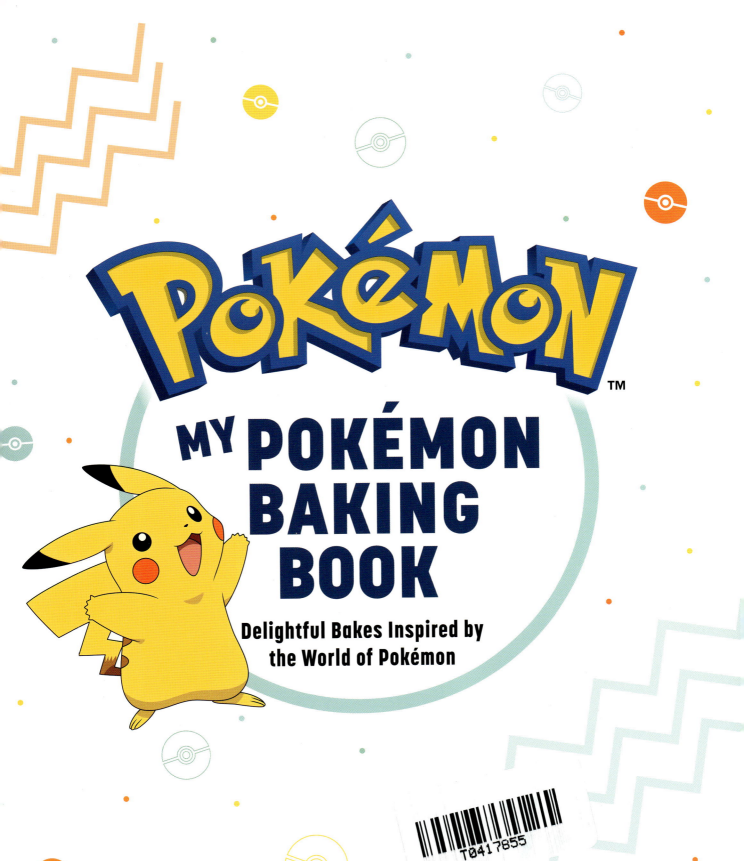

Pokémon™

MY POKÉMON BAKING BOOK

Delightful Bakes Inspired by the World of Pokémon

MY POKÉMON BAKING BOOK

Delightful Bakes Inspired by the World of Pokémon

Jarrett Melendez

INSIGHT
EDITIONS

SAN RAFAEL · LOS ANGELES · LONDON

Contents

Introduction

For decades, the Pokémon universe has inspired millions to be the very best they can be through embarking on adventures, building relationships with other Trainers, practicing and training, and, of course, collecting lots and lots of different types of Pokémon. Only by building a strong team of varied Pokémon can you achieve your goals, and that requires knowledge and patience—both of which are also needed for baking.

Just like the Pokémon you train, you'll need to learn lots of skills and techniques to master the recipes in this book. But don't worry: Most recipes contained within are family-friendly and suitable for bakers of any skill level. You'll find simple cookies and brownies all the way up to challenging bakes, like a soufflé inspired by the Legendary Pokémon Koraidon, that might require a little help and a watchful eye.

The techniques of each bake aren't the only things that are wide and varied. Each recipe is inspired by different Pokémon throughout the generations and across the various regions of the Pokémon universe. There are recipes inspired by Fire-type Pokémon that contain warming spices like cinnamon and ginger to heat your bellies and hearts. Other recipes are inspired by Ice-type Pokémon, with ingredients like mint for a refreshing blast of flavor on your palate. You'll discover recipes inspired by Ground- and Rock-type Pokémon that are packed with chocolate or nuts for a dense, rich experience that'll leave you full (yet still wanting more!). Some recipes even reflect the different regions in the Pokémon universe, such as Comfey's Tropical Pavlova, which feels right at home in the tropical setting of Alola, as well as Chespin's Raspberry Pistachio Napoleons, which look elegant enough to grace the tables of the finest castles in Kalos.

The goal of this book is to capture the sense of wonder and adventure found in the Pokémon universe and transport it to the world of baking. Just like beating a tough Gym Leader in a Pokémon battle, there's nothing more satisfying than pulling off a challenging bake. So fire up the oven, get out your mixing bowls and whisks, and let's get baking!

Ingredient Guide

Black Cocoa Powder: Prized for its deep, dark color, this type of cocoa powder turns baked goods a dramatic shade and fills them with an even deeper chocolate flavor. During processing, it is treated with an alkaline solution, which reduces the natural acidity in the chocolate, creating a smoother consistency and flavor. It can be found in specialty baking supply shops and online.

Butterfly Pea Flower Powder: This adorable little plant gets its name from the pea family it belongs to and its delicate blossoms shaped like—you guessed it—butterflies. Prized for the delicate blue color they impart on drinks and food, the blossoms are often used to make tea. This all-natural food coloring bestows both a soft blue color and a light floral flavor. The powder can be found in health food stores and specialty grocery stores and online.

Freeze-dried Fruit Powders: Throughout this book, you'll see blueberry powder, pineapple powder, raspberry powder, and strawberry powder used in recipes. Freeze-dried fruits are becoming more popular with home bakers because they have a much more concentrated flavor, so you can use less while imparting more flavor than when baking with fruit jams or purées. While it is more common to find freeze-dried whole fruits in grocery stores and big-box department stores, the pre-powdered forms are easy to find in health food stores and online. If you can find only the whole-fruit versions, simply grind them down in a spice grinder, with a mortar and pestle, or with a trusty zippered storage bag and rolling pin, and sift. If you have any leftover powder or larger crumbles, you can use them as snacks, blend them into smoothies, or decorate your bakes with them.

Pistachio Paste: Made from peeled, roasted pistachios, this paste is packed with natural pistachio flavor. Pistachio paste is notoriously difficult to make at home because you *have* to peel each pistachio individually, by hand (there's no simple or mechanized way to do it!). Fortunately, pistachio paste can be found in specialty shops and online.

Praline Paste: Made from toasted, caramelized hazelnuts and almonds that are ground into a fine paste, this specialty ingredient imparts delicious nutty flavor, caramel notes, and richness to anything you add it to. It can be found in high-end grocery stores and specialty baking shops and online.

Vanilla Powder: Every single part of the vanilla bean is packed with vanilla flavor, including the waxy outer pod. Many vanilla extract producers have started drying and powdering these pods for use in baking to reduce waste and stretch each of these rare and difficult-to-grow beans a bit more. Using vanilla powder in recipes adds larger brown flecks of color and a bit of texture while imparting the same complex vanilla flavor as extract or paste. That said, extract and paste are perfectly acceptable substitutes for any recipe that calls for vanilla powder. Vanilla powder is becoming more readily available in many grocery stores and specialty baking shops, as well as online.

Kanto Region

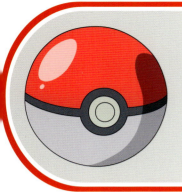

Poké Ball
Conchas

One of the most important tools in any Pokémon Trainer's backpack is the Poké Ball. The sweetness of these traditional rolls rivals the sweet taste of victory you feel when catching a new Pokémon pal. Try using different colors of dye and patterns to make a variety of Poké Balls, or stick with the basic red-and-white design.

Difficulty: ● ● ● ○
Prep time: 40 minutes
Rest time: 2½ hours
Bake time: 1 hour
Yield: 12 conchas
Dietary notes: Vegetarian

Equipment: Stand mixer, hand mixer, half-sheet pans, scale, 4-inch cookie cutter, instant-read thermometer, wire cooling rack

Concha Dough

2½ teaspoons active dry yeast

½ cup whole milk, lukewarm

3 large eggs, room temperature

1 tablespoon vanilla paste

½ cup sugar

3 cups bread flour

1½ teaspoons kosher salt

8 tablespoons unsalted butter, softened

Cookie Topping

1 cup all-purpose flour

¾ cup powdered sugar, plus more for dusting

½ teaspoon kosher salt

8 tablespoons unsalted butter, melted and cooled

1 teaspoon vanilla extract

Red food coloring

1 large egg

Decorations

Black fondant

White chocolate buttons

1. Whisk together the active dry yeast and milk in a small bowl. Let sit for about 5 minutes, until foamy. If the mixture doesn't foam, the milk may be too warm. The ideal temperature should be between 100°F and 110°F. Otherwise, the yeast may be expired, and you may need to buy new yeast.

2. Add the yeast-and-milk mixture to the bowl of a stand mixer fitted with a dough hook. Add the eggs, vanilla paste, sugar, bread flour, and salt to the bowl and mix on low until moistened. Increase speed to medium and mix for 3 to 5 minutes until a loose dough forms.

3. Add the butter, 1 tablespoon at a time, allowing the butter to fully incorporate between each addition. When you've added all the butter, increase the mixer speed to medium-high and let mix for 15 to 20 minutes, until the dough is still tacky but pulls away from the sides of the bowl.

4. Cover the bowl and let sit in a warm place for about 1 hour, until the dough has doubled in volume and looks quite puffy.

note: This process, called proofing, gives your bread its airy texture and flavor. During the proofing process, the yeast eats the sugars in the dough and releases gas, stretching the gluten strands and making the dough puff up.

5. While the concha dough is rising, make the cookie topping. Mix the flour, powdered sugar, and salt in a medium bowl. Stir in the butter and vanilla until a soft dough forms.

6. Divide the cookie topping dough into two equal portions. Beat about 15 drops of red food coloring into one half of the dough with a handheld mixer until it is fully incorporated and looks homogenous. Divide both the white dough and the red dough into 6 equal portions, for a total of 12 balls of dough. Cover with plastic wrap and set aside.

continued on the next page

7. Line two half-sheet pans with parchment paper. Take out the concha dough, gently punch it down to deflate, and turn it out onto a generously floured surface. Weigh the dough with a digital scale and divide it into 12 equal portions. Working with one ball of dough at a time, shape the pieces into balls and then place them on your work surface. Cup your hand over the ball of dough, with your fingertips on the work surface. Move your cupped hand in a circular motion over the dough to tighten the surface and form a smooth ball. Move the shaped roll to one of the prepared pans. Repeat with the remaining dough, placing 6 rolls on each sheet pan.

8. Sandwich one ball of the cookie topping between two squares of parchment paper. Flatten with a heavy pot or skillet to form a round a bit larger than 4 inches across. Use a 4-inch cookie cutter to cut out a perfect circle. Cut the circle in half with a sharp knife. Repeat with all 12 balls of cookie topping.

9. In a small bowl, beat the remaining egg together with 1 tablespoon water. Brush the tops of all the concha dough balls with the egg wash. Top each piece of concha dough with one semicircle of white cookie topping, and one semicircle of red cookie topping, overlapping them by about ½ inch.

10. Let the prepared dough rise, uncovered, until doubled in size, 1 to 1½ hours. In the last half-hour of rising, preheat the oven to 325°F.

11. When the dough has risen, place one sheet pan of conchas in the fridge, and bake the other sheet pan of conchas for 25 to 30 minutes until they are golden brown and the internal temperature registers at 195°F on an instant-read thermometer. Remove from the oven and let cool on the pan for 10 minutes before transferring the conchas to a wire rack to cool completely. Repeat with the remaining sheet pan of conchas.

12. Knead the black fondant separately on a clean, dry surface until smooth and pliable. Lightly dust the surface with powdered sugar and roll out the fondant (about $\frac{1}{10}$ inch thick). Cut the fondant into 12 thin strips that are as long as your conchas and about ½ inch wide.

13. Cut out 12 black circles (about 1½ inches in diameter). Place a black band over the middle of each concha, where the red and white halves meet, then arrange a black circle in the center of the concha. Place a white chocolate button in the center of each black circle, then serve.

Charmander
Brown Butter Marmalade Financiers

Brown butter gives this bright, citrusy dessert a nutty, toasty flavor, and these round, miniature cakes are loaded with a beautiful, bright orange marmalade—as bright as this beloved Fire-type Pokémon! Of course, you can make brown butter by leaving it next to a Charmander's tail, but we recommend using a saucepan on your stove instead.

Difficulty: ● ● ○ ○
Prep time: 15 minutes
Bake time: 20 minutes
Yield: 12 financiers
Dietary notes: Vegetarian

Equipment: 12-cup muffin tin, small saucepan

Financiers
8 tablespoons unsalted butter
2 cups almond flour
¾ cup all-purpose flour
¾ teaspoon kosher salt
½ cup sugar
6 egg whites
2 teaspoons vanilla extract
½ teaspoon almond extract

Marmalade Filling
6 tablespoons marmalade
1 teaspoon ground ginger
1 tablespoon freshly grated ginger

1. Preheat the oven to 375°F. Lightly grease a standard 12-cup muffin tin.

2. Heat the butter in a small saucepan over medium heat. Cook, swirling the pan occasionally, until the solids turn golden brown, about 7 to 10 minutes. Let cool slightly.

3. Whisk together the almond flour, all-purpose flour, salt, and sugar in a large bowl. Stir in the brown butter.

4. Beat the egg whites, along with the vanilla and almond extracts, in a small bowl until quite foamy, about 1 to 2 minutes. Stir this into the flour mixture. Divide the batter among all 12 cups in the muffin tin. Set aside.

5. Prepare the marmalade filling by adding the marmalade, ground ginger, and fresh ginger to a small saucepan and heating over medium-low until runny, about 3 to 5 minutes. Stir to combine.

6. Use a wet finger to make a divot in the center of each financier. Add 1½ teaspoons marmalade filling to each financier. Bake for 20 minutes until golden brown. Let cool in the pan for 10 minutes before transferring to a wire rack to cool. Serve warm or at room temperature.

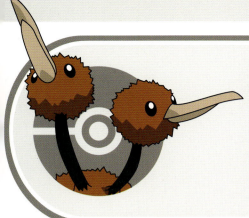

Doduo
Chocolate Macaroons

These chocolate macaroons are a great snack when you need a little energy boost. While these macaroons may not give you the ability to run as fast as a Doduo or stay alert while asleep, they pack a chocolatey punch along with lots of toasted coconut flavor that's sure to give you powerful strides!

Difficulty: ● ○ ○ ○
Prep time: 10 minutes
Bake time: 20 to 25 minutes
Yield: 24 macaroons
Dietary notes: Gluten-free, nondairy, vegetarian

Equipment: Half-sheet pan, 2-tablespoon cookie scoop, microwave, 2 piping bags

Macaroons

4 ounces bittersweet chocolate, melted and cooled

¼ cup cocoa powder, plus more for dusting

1 cup sugar

½ teaspoon kosher salt

1½ teaspoons vanilla powder or extract

4 egg whites

3 cups unsweetened shredded coconut, lightly toasted

Decorations

Slivered almonds

Black and white candy melts

1. Preheat the oven to 350°F. Line a half-sheet pan with parchment paper. Stir together the chocolate, cocoa powder, sugar, kosher salt, and vanilla in a large bowl.

2. Vigorously beat the egg whites in a separate large bowl until frothy, about 1 to 2 minutes. Stir into the chocolate mixture. Fold in the toasted coconut until well incorporated.

3. Use a 2-tablespoon cookie scoop to portion 24 macaroons onto the prepared sheet pan. If you don't have a cookie scoop, measure out 2 tablespoons of mix for each cookie and roll it into a ball with your hands. Leave about an inch between each cookie—they will not spread or rise, so it's okay to fit all 24 on the same sheet pan.

4. Bake for 20 to 25 minutes until the cookies are set but not fully dry. Let cool for about 10 minutes, then dust with additional cocoa powder to coat if desired. Carefully insert 2 almond slivers into each one to form Doduo's beak. If the almond slivers break too easily, poke two holes into each macaroon with a chopstick, then insert the almond slivers into the holes. Let cool completely and serve.

5. Place the black candy melts in a microwave-safe bowl. Heat for 30 seconds at a time until the candy is fully melted. Stir until smooth, then pour into a piping bag.

6. Cut off the tip of the piping bag to create a small opening. Pipe 48 small circles onto the parchment and let set for a few minutes. These will be Doduo's eyes.

7. Repeat step 5 with the white candy melts in a clean piping bag. Cut off the tip of the piping bag to create a very small opening and pipe a small white dot on the set black eyes to complete Doduo's eyes.

8. Assemble each macaroon using the eyes you made with the candy melts. Let the macaroons cool completely, then serve.

Pikachu
Tropical Cupcakes

These brightly colored cupcakes are full of delicious tropical flavor. The coconut cupcake base is as sweet as a Pikachu's face, while the pineapple frosting is reminiscent of the iconic Mouse Pokémon and packed with enough tartness to give your tongue a little zap. Eating just one of these cupcakes will put you in the mood to surf the waves!

Difficulty: ● ● ○ ○
Prep time: 45 minutes
Bake time: 30 minutes
Yield: 12 cupcakes
Dietary notes: Vegetarian

Equipment: 12-cup muffin tin, stand mixer, wire cooling rack, hand mixer, five piping bags (one with ½-inch round tip), sheet pan

Cupcakes

2 cups all-purpose flour

¾ teaspoon baking powder

½ teaspoon baking soda

½ teaspoon kosher salt

16 tablespoons unsalted butter, room temperature

1¼ cups sugar

3 large eggs, room temperature

2 teaspoons vanilla extract

¾ cup buttermilk, room temperature

8 ounces unsweetened shredded coconut, toasted

Frosting

2 cups powdered sugar

8 tablespoons unsalted butter, softened

3 tablespoons pineapple powder

2 teaspoons lemon juice

2 tablespoons heavy cream

Yellow food coloring

Decorations

Black, white, yellow, and red candy melts

To make the cupcakes:

1. Preheat the oven to 325°F. Line a standard muffin tin with 12 paper cupcake liners.

2. Whisk together the flour, baking powder, baking soda, and kosher salt in a medium bowl until combined. Set aside.

3. Cream together the butter and sugar in the bowl of a stand mixer fitted with a paddle attachment. Beat at medium speed until light and fluffy, about 5 to 7 minutes. Add the eggs, one at a time, beating until fully incorporated before adding the next egg. Add the vanilla and beat to combine.

4. Reduce the mixer speed to low. Add ⅓ of the flour mixture, beat to combine, then add ⅓ of the buttermilk. Repeat with the remaining flour mixture and buttermilk. Turn off the mixer, and fold in the toasted coconut with a rubber spatula.

5. Pour the batter into the prepared muffin tin. Bake for 25 to 30 minutes until the cupcakes are golden brown on top and a cake tester or toothpick inserted into the cakes comes out clean. Let the cupcakes cool in the pan for 10 minutes before transferring them to a wire rack to cool completely.

To make the frosting:

6. Add the powdered sugar, butter, and pineapple powder to a large bowl. Mix with a handheld mixer on low speed until the powdered sugar is moistened, then increase the speed to medium-high and beat for about 8 minutes, until light and fluffy. Add the lemon juice and mix for about 1 minute to combine, then add the heavy cream 1 tablespoon at a time and mix until perfectly smooth. Mix in yellow food coloring as needed to achieve the perfect Pikachu color.

note: If you can't find freeze-dried pineapple or pineapple powder, omit the heavy cream and use 2 tablespoons of pineapple juice. If using pineapple juice, make sure to bring to a simmer for a few minutes in a small saucepan to denature the enzymes, or your frosting will curdle. You could also use previously frozen juice.

continued on the next page

To assemble:

7. Add the frosting to a piping bag fitted with a ½-inch round tip. Hold the piping bag over each cupcake and pipe a medium-size swirl of frosting onto the cupcake. Flip the cupcake upside down onto a piece of wax paper and carefully smush the cupcake down, spreading the frosting flat across the top of the cupcake. If necessary, use a knife or an offset spatula to smooth the edges of the frosting around the cupcake. Chill the cupcakes in the fridge for 5 to 10 minutes.

8. Line a sheet pan with parchment paper.

9. Place the black candy melts in a microwave-safe bowl. Heat for 30 seconds at a time until the candy is fully melted. Stir until smooth, then pour into a piping bag, reserving some for dipping (see step 12).

10. Cut off the tip of the piping bag to create a small opening. Pipe 24 circles onto the parchment and let set for a few minutes. These will be Pikachu's eyes. Use the remaining black melts to pipe 12 noses and 12 mouths.

11. Repeat the melting instructions in step 9 with the white candy melts in a clean piping bag. Cut off the tip of the piping bag to create a very small opening and pipe a small white dot on the set black eyes to complete Pikachu's eyes.

12. Repeat the melting instructions in step 9 with the yellow candy melts. Pipe 24 long, thin, ovular shapes that are about 2 to 2½ inches long and that follow the shape of Pikachu's ears, becoming widest in the middle and tapering to a point at the end. These will be Pikachu's ears. Let set. When they are set, dip the ends in the reserved black candy melt at an angle, so that the black part takes up about a third of the ear and is longer on the outside of the ear compared to the inside.

13. Repeat the melting instructions in step 9 with the red candy melts. Pipe 24 small circles, larger than the eyes, to create the red dots on Pikachu's cheeks.

14. Assemble each cupcake using the eyes, noses, mouths, and cheek dots you made with the candy melts. Place the eyes in the center vertically, with the ears sticking out of the top of the cupcake above the eyes at an angle. Place the two cheeks on the lower curves of the face below the eyes. Place the nose between the eyes horizontally, and between the eyes and cheeks vertically. Finally, place the mouth between the cheeks, set just above their center.

Ponyta
Cinnamon Panna Cotta

The not-so-secret ingredient in this sweetened cream dessert is cinnamon, which gives the custard a pleasant warmth. It's cool to the touch, which may seem strange for a Fire-type Pokémon—but Ponyta's fiery mane won't burn you, either, after it learns to trust you! Top your panna cotta with candied orange zest shaped in a flame motif for a flashy finish.

Difficulty: ● ● ○ ○
Prep time: 20 minutes
Cook time: 15 minutes
Chill time: 5 to 29 hours
Yield: Serves 6
Dietary notes: Gluten-free

Equipment: Medium saucepan, six ½-cup dessert dishes

Base

1½ cups heavy cream

1 cup whole milk

¼ cup sugar

¼ teaspoon salt

4 cinnamon sticks

Gelatin Mixture

2 teaspoons gelatin granules

½ cup whole milk

Decoration

Candied orange peel

1. Whisk the heavy cream, whole milk, sugar, and salt in a medium saucepan. Add the cinnamon sticks and cook over medium heat for about 5 to 7 minutes, stirring occasionally, until the liquid just begins to steam. Remove from heat and let steep for at least 1 hour at room temperature, or for up to 24 hours covered and chilled in the fridge.

2. Prepare the gelatin by sprinkling the gelatin granules over the ½ cup whole milk. Let the gelatin granules hydrate for 5 minutes. Stir to combine, then add the milk-and-gelatin mixture to the saucepan with the chilled heavy cream mixture. Heat over medium heat until just beginning to simmer, about 6 to 8 minutes, but do not let it come to a boil. Remove from heat.

3. Divide the mixture among six ½-cup dessert dishes. Cover with plastic wrap and chill for at least 4 hours to set.

4. Cut the candied orange peel into spear shapes of different lengths. Gently place on top of the set panna cotta, arranging the spears to look like the end of Ponyta's flaming tail. Serve chilled.

Shellder
Madeleines

Did you know that Shellder sometimes make pearls out of the sand they accumulate at the bottom of the ocean? Fortunately, you won't have to worry about chomping into a pearl when you dig into these tender little shell-shaped cakes, made with a special madeleine pan to create the distinctive shape. This classic French dessert is sweetened with honey and spiked with orange zest for a delicately floral, citrusy flavor, which is rounded out with a purple-tinted white chocolate dipping sauce to emulate the beloved Bivalve Pokémon.

Difficulty: ● ● ● ○
Prep time: 15 minutes
Bake time: 10 to 12 minutes
Yield: 12 madeleines
Dietary notes: Vegetarian

Equipment: 12-cake madeleine pan, piping bag, microwave

Madeleines

1 cup all-purpose flour, plus more for dusting

1 teaspoon baking powder

¾ teaspoon kosher salt

2 large eggs, room temperature

2 tablespoons honey

Zest of 1 orange

7 tablespoons unsalted butter, melted, plus more for the pan

White Chocolate Dipping Sauce

6 ounces white chocolate

1 tablespoon butterfly pea flower powder, or a couple drops of blue food coloring

1 drop red food coloring

1. Preheat the oven to 400°F. Generously butter a 12-cake madeleine pan. Dust with flour, then tap out the excess.

2. Whisk together the flour, baking powder, and salt in a small bowl. In a medium bowl, beat the eggs, honey, and orange zest until smooth. Stir in the flour mixture. Continue stirring as you slowly drizzle the butter into the bowl until it's fully incorporated.

3. Pour the batter into a piping bag. If the batter is quite runny, chill in the fridge for at least an hour. Otherwise, cut off the tip of the bag to make a ½-inch opening, then pipe the batter into the prepared madeleine pan and bake for 10 to 12 minutes, until the cakes are golden brown.

4. As the madeleines bake, prepare the dipping sauce. Add the white chocolate to a small microwave-safe bowl. Microwave for 30 seconds, stir, and repeat until the chocolate is fully melted and smooth. Stir in the butterfly pea flower powder and red food coloring a little at a time until the chocolate looks homogenous and the purple Shellder color is achieved. Serve alongside warm madeleines.

Johto Region

Phanpy Orange Cream Tartlets

Togepi Confetti Mug Cake

Chikorita Cheesy
Pesto Brioche Rolls

Igglybuff Chocolate
Raspberry Cupcakes

Delibird Red Velvet
Cake with Peppermint
Cream Cheese Frosting

Blissey Strawberry Twists

Magby Spicy Cherry
Tomato Galette

Phanpy
Orange Cream Tartlets

These tiny tarts have an orange-flavored crust and a colorful vanilla custard filling. We finish with a strip of candied orange peel to tie the flavors together and match the cute orange stripe on Phanpy's trunk. Like Phanpy, these tarts may be small, but they pack a (citrusy) punch—and, thankfully, these tarts won't send you flying!

Difficulty: ● ● ○ ○
Prep time: 15 minutes
Chill time: 3 hours
Cook time: 35 minutes
Yield: 12 mini tarts
Dietary notes: Vegetarian

Equipment: Medium saucier, fine mesh strainer, food processor, 12-cup muffin tin, 4-inch cookie cutter, wire cooling rack, offset spatula

Custard
3 large egg whites
¾ cup sugar
1 teaspoon vanilla extract
¾ cup heavy cream
¾ cup whole milk
2 tablespoons unsalted butter
2 to 3 drops blue food coloring (optional)

Crust
1½ cups all-purpose flour
¼ cup powdered sugar
½ teaspoon kosher salt
2 teaspoons orange zest
8 tablespoons unsalted butter, cut into ½-inch cubes
1 tablespoon orange juice
2 tablespoons heavy cream
Red and yellow food coloring (optional)

Decoration
Dried papaya, cut into thin 2-inch-long strips

To make the custard:

1. To make the custard, add the egg whites, sugar, and vanilla to a medium bowl. Vigorously whisk the mixture until it's pale and thick.

2. Bring the heavy cream and milk to a bare simmer over medium heat in a medium saucier, stirring occasionally. Begin whisking the egg white mixture. While whisking continuously, pour in the hot milk mixture in a slow, gentle drizzle, a little bit at a time, until fully incorporated.

> **note:** Sauciers have a curved bottom, which makes them preferable when a mixture will likely get trapped in the edges of a straight-sided saucepan. A saucepan is okay to use if you don't have a saucier, but you'll have to be extra vigilant and thorough with stirring so that the mixture doesn't get trapped in the edges and burn.

3. Return the mixture to the saucier and warm it over medium-low heat, whisking constantly, until the mixture thickens and begins to bubble. Once you see the first bubble, set a 1-minute timer and continue whisking. When the minute is up, remove from heat and pour through a fine mesh strainer set over a medium bowl. Whisk in the butter and blue food coloring (if using) until smooth. Cover with plastic wrap, pushing the wrap directly onto the custard (to prevent a skin from forming) and chill for at least 3 hours.

To make the crust:

4. Add the flour, powdered sugar, salt, orange zest, and butter to the bowl of a food processor. Pulse until the mixture resembles wet sand. Tip the contents of the bowl into a large mixing bowl.

5. Stir together the orange juice, heavy cream, 1 drop of red food coloring, and 5 drops of yellow food coloring (if using) in a small bowl. Add to the flour mixture and stir with a wooden spoon until a firm dough forms. Wrap in plastic wrap and chill for at least 1 hour.

continued on the next page

To finish and assemble:

6. Preheat the oven to 350°F. Lightly grease a standard 12-cup muffin tin.

7. Begin assembling the tarts in the last 30 minutes of the custard's chill time. Place the prepared tart dough on a lightly floured surface. Roll out to a thickness of about ¼ inch, then use a 4-inch cookie cutter to punch out 12 rounds. If necessary, knead the scraps together, reroll to a thickness of ¼ inch, and repeat until you have 12 rounds.

8. Gently press the dough into the cups of the muffin tin, making sure the dough is uniform and flat against the insides of the cups.

9. Line each tart shell with a square of foil and fill with uncooked rice or beans—this will prevent the tart shells from puffing up in the oven. Bake for 15 minutes. Remove the beans (or rice) and foil, then bake for 5 to 8 more minutes until golden brown. Let cool in the pans for 15 minutes, then loosen with a thin knife to remove. Transfer to a wire cooling rack to cool completely.

10. Fill each tart shell with the cooled custard. Smooth over the tops with an offset spatula, then place a strip of dried papaya across the center of each tart. Transfer the finished tarts to a plate or platter, cover with foil or plastic wrap, and keep chilled until ready to serve.

Togepi
Confetti Mug Cake

This petite cake is simple and quick to make, perfect for those times when your sweet tooth strikes and you need dessert in a hurry. This sweet, vanilla-flavored cake is full of brightly colored sprinkles, to emulate Togepi's cute appearance. It's also warm and comforting right out of the microwave, like the compassion and happiness that Togepi stores in its shell.

Difficulty: ● ○ ○ ○
Prep time: 5 minutes
Cook time: 2 minutes
Yield: 1 mug cake
Dietary notes: Vegetarian

Equipment: 12-ounce mug, microwave

Mug Cake

1 tablespoon unsalted butter

2 tablespoons sugar

½ teaspoon vanilla

¼ teaspoon kosher salt

1 tablespoon whole milk

1 large egg

¼ cup all-purpose flour

¼ teaspoon baking powder

1½ tablespoons sprinkles

To Serve

Vanilla ice cream

Sprinkles

1. Add the butter to a 12-ounce mug. Heat in the microwave on high in 5-second intervals until the butter is soft and beginning to melt. Stir in the sugar, vanilla, salt, and milk. Beat in the egg until smooth, about 1 minute. Stir in the flour, baking powder, and sprinkles.

2. Microwave for 1 minute to 1 minute and 20 seconds until the cake is puffed and set. Serve warm with a scoop of vanilla ice cream on top and additional sprinkles, as desired.

Chikorita
Cheesy Pesto Brioche Rolls

These tender brioche rolls are packed with cheese and bright, flavorful pesto, making them great for an afternoon snack or as an accompaniment to your favorite pasta dish. Each one is topped with a fresh basil leaf while the rolls are still warm, which gives off a pleasant smell, just like the leaf on Chikorita's head.

Difficulty: ● ● ○ ○
Prep time: 30 minutes
Rest time: 3½ hours
Bake time: 30 minutes
Yield: 12 rolls
Dietary notes: Vegetarian

Equipment: Stand mixer, 12-cup muffin tin, wire cooling rack

Brioche

1 cup whole milk, lukewarm

4 cups all-purpose flour, plus more for dusting

1 tablespoon instant yeast

2½ teaspoons kosher salt

2 tablespoons sugar

3 large eggs

8 tablespoons unsalted butter, softened

Filling

One 6-ounce jar pesto

8 ounces shredded mozzarella cheese

¼ cup grated Parmesan cheese

12 fresh basil leaves

note: If you're unsure whether the dough is ready in step 2, tear off a small chunk. Stretch the dough—if you can stretch it enough to see through it without the dough tearing, it's ready to go. If the dough tears, continue mixing for 5 more minutes, then test it again. (This is called the windowpane test.)

1. Add the milk, flour, yeast, salt, and sugar to the bowl of a stand mixer fitted with a dough hook attachment. Mix on low until a shaggy dough forms (the dough will be lumpy, with no dry flour remaining). Add the eggs, one at a time, mixing continuously; wait for each egg to completely incorporate before adding the next one. Increase the mixer speed to medium and mix until the dough is smooth, about 5 minutes.

2. Add the butter 2 tablespoons at a time, allowing the butter to incorporate between each addition. Mix for about 15 more minutes, until the dough is smooth, glossy, and elastic.

3. Place the dough in a lightly oiled bowl and cover. Let rise for 1½ to 2 hours until the dough is quite puffy and has nearly doubled in volume. Lightly grease a standard muffin tin.

4. Tip out the dough onto a lightly floured surface and gently press it down to deflate. Sprinkle a small amount of flour over the top of the dough, then roll it out into a 13-by-16-inch rectangle.

5. Spread the pesto over the surface of the dough, leaving a 1-inch border along one of the shorter sides. Sprinkle the mozzarella and Parmesan cheese over the pesto, leaving the same 1-inch border clean. Starting at the short side *without* the clean border, roll the dough into a tight log, ending at the clean border. Pinch the dough to seal.

6. Trim ½ inch off each end of the log, then cut it into twelve 1-inch-thick discs. Place 1 disc in each prepared muffin cup. Lightly cover the muffin pan with plastic wrap and let the dough rise for 1 to 1½ hours, until it's quite puffy. Toward the end of the rising time, preheat the oven to 350°F.

7. Bake for 25 to 30 minutes or until the internal temperature registers 195°F on an instant-read thermometer inserted into the center of each roll.

8. Let the rolls cool for 5 minutes in the pan before transferring them to a wire rack to cool until they're just warm enough to eat comfortably. Insert a fresh basil leaf into the center of each roll and take a calming breath of fresh, warm basil scent. Serve warm or at room temperature.

Igglybuff
Chocolate Raspberry Cupcakes

Igglybuff are known for releasing a sweet, calming aroma to soothe their foes and others around them. These cupcakes may not smell quite like Igglybuff, but this blend of chocolate and raspberry is just the sweet thing to soothe your nerves after a long, tough day.

Difficulty: ● ● ○ ○
Prep time: 15 minutes
Bake time: 25 minutes
Yield: 12 cupcakes
Dietary notes: Vegetarian

Equipment: 12-cup muffin tin, stand mixer, wire cooling rack, hand mixer, two piping bags (one with ½-inch round tip), microwave

Cupcakes

1 cup all-purpose flour

½ cup cocoa powder

1 teaspoon baking powder

½ teaspoon baking soda

½ teaspoon kosher salt

1 teaspoon espresso powder

2 large eggs, room temperature

1 large egg yolk, room temperature

½ cup sugar

4 tablespoons unsalted butter, room temperature

¼ cup canola oil (or other neutral oil)

1 tablespoon vanilla extract

¾ cup sour cream

Frosting

2 cups powdered sugar

8 tablespoons unsalted butter, softened

1½ tablespoons raspberry powder or 3 tablespoons raspberry jam

1 teaspoon lemon juice

2 tablespoons heavy cream

2 ounces dark chocolate

note: To ensure neat spirals, you can also pipe the chocolate onto a sheet of parchment paper. Chill the chocolate in the refrigerator until the chocolate hardens (10 to 20 minutes), then carefully transfer to the top of the cupcake.

1. Preheat the oven to 350°F. Line a standard muffin tin with 12 paper cupcake liners. Whisk together the flour, cocoa powder, baking powder, baking soda, salt, and espresso powder in a large bowl.

2. Add the eggs, egg yolk, sugar, butter, oil, and vanilla to the bowl of a stand mixer fitted with a paddle attachment. Beat on medium for about 5 minutes, until smooth.

3. Reduce the mixer speed to low, then add half of the flour mixture and mix until just combined. Add the sour cream, mixing to combine. Add the remaining flour mixture and mix until no dry flour is visible. Scrape down the sides and bottom of the bowl with a rubber spatula to ensure that the batter is homogenous.

4. Divide the batter evenly among the 12 cupcake liners and bake for 20 to 25 minutes or until a cake tester comes out clean when inserted into the centers of the cupcakes. Let the cupcakes cool in the pan for 10 minutes before transferring them to a wire rack to cool completely.

5. Make the frosting while the cupcakes cool. Add the powdered sugar, butter, and raspberry powder to a large bowl. Mix with a handheld mixer on low speed until the powdered sugar is moistened, then increase the speed to medium-high and beat for about 8 minutes, until light and fluffy. Add the lemon juice and mix for about 1 minute to combine, then add the heavy cream 1 tablespoon at a time, mixing until perfectly smooth.

6. Add the frosting to a piping bag fitted with a ½-inch round tip. Pipe a round mound of frosting onto each cupcake. Flip the cupcake upside down onto a piece of wax paper and carefully smush the cupcake down, spreading the frosting flat across the top of the cupcake. If necessary, use a knife or an offset spatula to smooth the edges of the frosting around the cupcake. Chill the cupcakes in the fridge for 5 to 10 minutes.

7. Place the dark chocolate in a microwave-safe bowl. Heat for 30 seconds at a time, stirring each time, until the chocolate is melted and smooth. Pour the chocolate into a piping bag and let it cool slightly—it should still be liquid, but not hot, or the chocolate will melt the frosting.

8. Pipe a chocolate spiral on each cupcake for the spiral on Igglybuff's head.

Delibird
Red Velvet Cake with Peppermint Cream Cheese Frosting

Although most red velvet cakes are topped with plain cream cheese frosting, this one has peppermint for a nice cooling effect to match Delibird's Ice-type nature. Delibird store food in their tails, which they use as sacks. The sack on top of this cake is also full of, and made from, food—frosting, specifically. What's more, the size of this cake is perfect for sharing because the Delivery Pokémon generously shares its food with people and Pokémon alike.

Difficulty: ● ● ○ ○
Prep time: 30 minutes
Bake time: 30 minutes
Yield: Serves 12 to 16
Dietary notes: Vegetarian

Equipment: Two 8-inch round cake pans, stand mixer, wire cooling racks, hand mixer, offset spatula, food processor, piping bags with large round tip and small star tip

Cake

2 cups cake flour

3 tablespoons cocoa powder

1 teaspoon baking soda

2 eggs

1½ cups sugar

8 tablespoons unsalted butter, melted and cooled

1 teaspoon salt

1 tablespoon vinegar

1 tablespoon vanilla extract

1½ tablespoons red food coloring

1 cup buttermilk

Frosting

2 cups powdered sugar

16 ounces cream cheese, softened

8 tablespoons unsalted butter, softened

1 teaspoon vanilla extract

2 teaspoons peppermint extract

Decorations

Peppermint candies

Black and yellow sugar sprinkles (optional)

To make the cake:

1. Preheat the oven to 350°F. Grease two 8-inch cake pans, and line the bottoms with a circle of parchment paper. Grease the parchment paper.

2. Whisk together the cake flour, cocoa powder, and baking soda in a small bowl. Set aside.

3. Add the eggs and sugar to the bowl of a stand mixer fitted with a paddle attachment. Beat on medium until the mixture is pale and thick. Add the butter, salt, vinegar, vanilla, and red food coloring, mixing until combined.

4. Reduce the mixer speed to low and add ⅓ of the flour mixture. Mix until just combined, then add half the buttermilk. Repeat with the remaining flour mixture and buttermilk, making sure that the flour mixture is the last addition. Mix until no dry flour remains. Scrape the sides and bottom of the bowl with a rubber spatula to ensure that the batter is homogenous.

5. Divide the batter between the two cake pans. Smooth the top of the batter, then bake for 30 minutes or until a cake tester inserted into the center of the cakes comes out clean. Let the cakes cool for 15 minutes in the pans, then transfer them to a wire rack to cool completely.

To make the frosting:

6. Make the frosting as the cakes cool. Add the powdered sugar, cream cheese, butter, vanilla, and peppermint extract to a large bowl. Beat with a handheld mixer until completely smooth, about 10 minutes.

To decorate:

7. If the cakes have domed, use a long serrated knife to trim the domed top off each cake so they are flat and level. Place one of the cooled cakes on a plate and add 1 cup of frosting to the top. Spread into an even layer with an offset spatula, then place the second cake on top. Add 1 cup of frosting to the top and spread it evenly over the top and sides, adding more frosting as needed, but reserving some to decorate the top.

8. Crush peppermint candies in a food processor until they are relatively fine, but not powdered. (It's okay to have some larger crunchy bits.) Press the crushed candies into the frosting on the side of the cake.

9. Add about ¾ of the remaining frosting to a piping bag fitted with a large round tip. Pipe one 4-inch-tall mound in the middle of the top of the cake. This is the bottom of Delibird's sack.

10. Line a small baking sheet or plate with parchment paper. Add the remaining frosting to a small piping bag fitted with a small star tip. Pipe a smaller mound onto the parchment and freeze it for 15 minutes or until firm enough to handle without losing its shape.

11. Peel the frozen mound off the parchment paper, and then invert it onto the round mound on the cake. The flat side of the frozen mound should be facing up, creating the top half of Delibird's sack.

12. If desired, sprinkle black and yellow sugar sprinkles over the top of the cake around the sack. Cut and serve.

Blissey
Strawberry Twists

Blissey are kindhearted and love helping and healing others, whether human or other Pokémon. These sweet strawberry twists don't have any healing powers, but they're a lovely cure for a sweet tooth—and they're pink, just like Blissey! This recipe makes enough to share, in case you want to deliver joy to others as the Happiness Pokémon does.

Difficulty: ● ● ○ ○
Prep time: 35 minutes
Rest time: 2 hours
Bake time: 25 minutes
Yield: 12 rolls
Dietary notes: Vegetarian

Equipment: Stand mixer, pizza cutter, 12-cup muffin tin, wire cooling rack, wire mesh strainer

Twists

4 cups all-purpose flour

½ teaspoon kosher salt

1 cup milk

4 tablespoons unsalted butter, softened

2 teaspoons instant yeast

2 tablespoons maple syrup

2 eggs

4 ounces strawberry jam

To Finish

1 egg

Raw sugar

½ cup powdered sugar

1 tablespoon strawberry powder

Whipped cream

1. Add the flour, salt, milk, butter, yeast, and maple syrup to the bowl of a stand mixer fitted with a dough hook attachment. Mix on low until moistened, then increase the speed to medium and mix until a shaggy dough forms (the dough will be lumpy, with no dry flour remaining).

2. Add 1 egg to the bowl and allow the mixer to run until the egg is fully incorporated. Repeat with the remaining egg. Increase speed to medium-high and knead for 15 more minutes.

3. Cover the bowl and set it in a warm spot in the kitchen for 1 hour or until the dough has doubled in volume.

note: If you're unsure whether the dough is ready, tear off a small chunk. Stretch the dough—if you can stretch it enough to see through it without the dough tearing, it's ready to go. If the dough tears, continue mixing for 5 more minutes, then test it again. (This is called the windowpane test.)

4. Turn out the dough onto a floured surface. Press down on the dough gently to deflate, then roll it into a 12-by-24-inch rectangle. Spread the strawberry jam over the surface, leaving a ½-inch border around the dough. Lightly wet the border with damp fingers, then fold the dough in half into a 12-by-12-inch square, firmly pressing the edges to seal.

5. Use a pizza cutter to cut the folded dough into twelve 1-inch-wide strips. Let the dough rest while you grease a standard muffin tin.

6. Hold the dough with one short end in each hand. Twist the dough strands together, then coil the dough into one of the prepared muffin tin cups, tucking the ends underneath the coil. Repeat with the remaining strips of dough.

continued on the next page

7. Loosely cover the muffin tin with greased plastic wrap and let the dough rise for 1 hour, or until it's quite puffy and has roughly doubled in volume. Toward the end of this hour, preheat the oven to 350°F.

8. Beat the egg with 1 tablespoon water. Brush the tops of each roll with the egg mixture, then sprinkle liberally with raw sugar. Bake for 20 to 25 minutes or until an instant-read thermometer registers 195°F when inserted into the center of the rolls.

9. Let the twists cool for 10 minutes in the pan, then transfer them to a wire rack to cool completely. To finish, sift ½ cup powdered sugar with 1 tablespoon strawberry powder over a bowl. Transfer to a wire mesh strainer and sift over the tops of the cooled rolls to coat them in a sweet strawberry-flavored powder. Top each roll with a dollop of whipped cream, sprinkle more powder sugar if desired, and serve.

Magby
Spicy Cherry Tomato Galette

Galettes are a great way to teach new bakers how to make pie crust. These are more like a freeform pie with no pie plate, but they follow the same basic recipe as a pie: crust and filling. The filling on this pie is savory, with a nice touch of heat and smoky flavor to match Magby's fiery nature, and the cherry tomatoes piled in the center look like Magby's head poking out of the center of the galette.

Difficulty: ● ● ○ ○
Prep time: 20 minutes
Rest time: 1 hour
Bake time: 35 minutes
Yield: 1 galette, serves 8
Dietary notes: Vegetarian

Equipment: Food processor, half-sheet pan, wire cooling rack

Crust
1¼ cups all-purpose flour
¼ cup semolina
¼ cup grated Parmesan cheese
8 tablespoons butter, cut into ½-inch cubes
½ teaspoon kosher salt

Filling
1 cup ricotta cheese
1 teaspoon lemon zest
½ teaspoon kosher salt
¼ teaspoon black pepper
½ teaspoon garlic powder
¼ teaspoon onion powder
¼ teaspoon oregano
2 large eggs, divided
1 pound cherry tomatoes, halved
½ teaspoon kosher salt
½ teaspoon smoked paprika
¼ teaspoon cayenne
1 tablespoon Calabrian chilis
1 tablespoon olive oil
Smoked flaky sea salt

1. Add the flour, semolina, Parmesan cheese, butter, and salt to the bowl of a food processor. Pulse until the mixture resembles wet sand. Tip the mixture into a bowl and add 1 to 2 tablespoons of cold water. Mix to form a soft dough, shape into a disc, wrap in plastic wrap, and chill in the fridge for 1 hour.

2. Meanwhile, prepare the filling. Add the ricotta cheese, lemon zest, salt, pepper, garlic powder, onion powder, oregano, and one of the eggs to a medium bowl. Whisk with a fork until smooth.

3. In a separate large bowl, add the cherry tomatoes, salt, smoked paprika, cayenne, Calabrian chilis, and olive oil. Toss to coat. Set aside.

4. Preheat the oven to 425°F. Line a half-sheet pan with parchment paper.

5. Place the prepared dough on a floured surface. Roll out the dough to a circle with a thickness of about ¼ inch. Transfer the dough to the prepared sheet pan. Spread the ricotta filling in the center of the dough, leaving about a 2-inch border of clean dough around the filling.

6. Spoon the tomato filling over the ricotta mixture, piling a few tomatoes higher in the center to form the top of Magby's head. Fold the dough up over the filling, pleating every 3 or 4 inches. Beat the remaining egg together with 1 tablespoon water and brush it on the top of the crust, then sprinkle smoked sea salt over the crust and filling.

7. Bake the galette for 30 to 35 minutes, until the tomatoes burst and the filling is bubbling. Cool on the pan for 15 minutes. Serve while still warm, or transfer to a wire rack to cool completely before serving.

note: If you can't find Calabrian chilis, use 1 tablespoon chopped chipotle peppers in adobo.

Hoenn Region

Seedot Black Sesame
Swirl Cake

Zigzagoon Mocha Éclairs

Taillow Chocolate Cherry
Olive Oil Cake

Whismur Lemon-Lavender Bars

Spoink Black Sesame
Cream Puffs

Flygon Pan Pizza

Seedot
Black Sesame Swirl Cake

Seedot love to prank other Pokémon by pretending to be nuts hanging in trees. You won't find this coffee cake hanging around in any trees, but the black sesame paste, almond extract, and crunchy sesame topping make it taste about as yummy as the nuts Seedot pretend to be.

Difficulty: ● ● ○ ○
Prep time: 15 minutes
Bake time: 35 minutes
Yield: Serves 12 to 16
Dietary notes: Vegetarian

Equipment: 9-inch tube pan, stand mixer, microwave, wire cooling rack, piping bag

Cake

2 cups all-purpose flour

1 teaspoon baking powder

½ teaspoon baking soda

½ teaspoon kosher salt

½ teaspoon cinnamon

¼ teaspoon ground cardamom

¼ teaspoon ground nutmeg

10 tablespoons unsalted butter, softened

1 cup sugar

¼ cup black sesame paste

2 large eggs

2 teaspoons vanilla extract

½ teaspoon almond extract

1 cup plain yogurt (not Greek)

Streusel Topping

¾ cup packed light brown sugar

¾ cup all-purpose flour

1 teaspoon cinnamon

½ teaspoon cardamom

¼ teaspoon kosher salt

1 tablespoon black sesame seeds

1 tablespoon white sesame seeds

1 tablespoon black sesame paste

4 tablespoons unsalted butter, melted

Decoration

2 ounces dark chocolate

To make the cake:

1. Preheat the oven to 350°F. Grease a 9-inch tube pan. Whisk together the flour, baking powder, baking soda, salt, cinnamon, cardamom, and nutmeg in a medium bowl. Set aside.

2. Add the butter, sugar, and black sesame paste in the bowl of a stand mixer fitted with a paddle attachment. Cream together on medium speed until light and fluffy, about 5 to 7 minutes.

3. Add the eggs, one at a time, beating to incorporate before adding the next one. Mix in the vanilla and almond extracts.

4. Reduce the mixer speed to low. Add ⅓ of the flour mixture and beat to incorporate. Add half of the yogurt, beating to incorporate. Repeat with the remaining ⅔ of the flour mixture and half of the yogurt, beating until incorporated and no dry pockets of flour remain. Pour the batter into the prepared tube pan. Set aside.

To make the streusel topping:

5. Stir together the brown sugar, flour, cinnamon, cardamom, salt, and black and white sesame seeds in a medium bowl. In a separate small bowl, stir together the black sesame paste and the butter until smooth. If the sesame paste is stiff, microwave it for about 30 seconds before attempting to stir it with the butter.

6. Stir the butter-and-sesame-paste mixture into the brown sugar mixture until crumbly. Scatter over the top of the cake batter. Bake for 30 to 35 minutes. Let the cake cool in the pan for 10 to 15 minutes, then transfer it to a wire rack to cool completely.

To decorate:

7. Place the dark chocolate in a microwave-safe bowl. Heat for 30 seconds at a time, stirring each time, until the chocolate is melted and smooth. Pour the chocolate into a piping bag and snip off the end to create a small hole.

8. Pipe two concentric circles on the top of the cake to match the design on Seedot's head.

Zigzagoon
Mocha Éclairs

Zigzagoon are wonderfully curious Pokémon and move in a zigzag pattern between the things that catch their interest. These mocha éclairs not only feature a zigzag pattern on top, but they also pack a chocolatey punch. They taste so good and look so charming, you'll be running as fast as a Zigzagoon to grab a second serving!

Difficulty: ● ● ● ○
Prep time: 45 minutes
Bake time: 40 minutes
Rest time: 80 minutes
Chill time: 4 hours
Yield: 10 to 12 éclairs
Dietary notes: Vegetarian

Equipment: Medium saucepan, fine mesh strainer, medium saucier, instant-read thermometer, stand mixer, half-sheet pan, 4 piping bags (with large star tip, 2 flat tips, and filling tip), wire cooling rack

Mocha Crème Pâtissière

1½ cups whole milk

½ cup heavy cream

1½ teaspoons instant espresso powder

½ cup sugar

3 tablespoons cornstarch

4 large egg yolks

1 teaspoon vanilla extract

4 ounces dark chocolate, chopped

Choux Pastry

1 cup whole milk

6 tablespoons unsalted butter

1 tablespoon sugar

¾ teaspoon kosher salt

1 cup all-purpose flour, sifted

4 large eggs

Icing

1¼ teaspoons instant espresso powder

1¼ teaspoons hot water

1¼ cups powdered sugar

1¼ tablespoons light corn syrup

1¼ teaspoons vanilla extract

3 to 4 tablespoons heavy cream

note: For chocolate lovers, remove the espresso powder from the crème pâtissière and replace the espresso powder in the icing with cocoa powder.

To make the mocha crème pâtissière:

1. Bring the milk, heavy cream, and espresso powder to a bare simmer in a medium saucepan over medium heat, stirring occasionally. Remove from heat.

2. In a medium bowl, whisk together the sugar and cornstarch. Add the egg yolks and whisk until smooth. While whisking constantly, slowly pour the milk and cream mixture into the cornstarch mixture.

3. Pour this mixture back into the saucepan and return it to medium heat. Whisk constantly until the mixture begins to bubble. The moment you see it bubble, set a 1-minute timer and continue to whisk constantly. Remove from heat.

4. Add the vanilla and chocolate to a medium bowl, then set a fine mesh strainer over the bowl. Pour the crème pâtissière through the fine mesh strainer, pushing it through with a rubber spatula. Let the crème pâtissière sit for 3 to 5 minutes to allow the chocolate to melt, then stir. Let cool for 20 minutes at room temperature before covering it and chilling for at least 4 hours.

To make the choux pastry:

5. While the crème pâtissière chills, make the éclair shells. Bring the milk, butter, sugar, and salt to a boil in a medium saucier over high heat. Remove from heat and vigorously stir in the flour with a wooden spoon until smooth.

note: Sauciers have a curved bottom, which makes them preferable when a mixture will likely get trapped in the edges of a straight-sided saucepan. A saucepan is okay to use if you don't have a saucier, but you'll have to be extra vigilant and thorough with stirring so that the mixture doesn't get trapped in the edges and burn.

6. Return the saucier to high heat and continue stirring vigorously until an instant-read thermometer registers 170°F when inserted into the mixture.

continued on the next page

7. Dump the mixture into the bowl of a stand mixer fitted with a paddle attachment. Beat on medium speed until the temperature drops to 145°F or lower. Start taking the temperature after about 3 minutes, then continue beating for 1 minute at a time until the correct temperature is reached.

8. Add the eggs one at a time, beating at medium speed until fully incorporated before adding the next egg. Once all the eggs are in, stop the mixer, scrape down the sides, and beat on medium speed for another 5 to 10 seconds until fully mixed.

9. Preheat the oven to 375°F, and line a half-sheet pan with parchment.

10. Transfer the choux batter to a large piping bag fitted with a large star tip. To keep the parchment from moving as you work, pipe a small blob of choux pastry under all four corners of the parchment.

11. Pipe ten to twelve 4-by-1½-inch logs onto the parchment. Bake for 40 minutes, until the éclairs are a deep golden brown and well puffed. Turn off the oven and prop open the door with a wooden spoon, allowing the éclairs to sit for another 20 to 30 minutes in the warm oven. Transfer the éclairs to a wire rack to cool completely.

To make the icing:

8. Stir together the instant espresso with very hot water in a small bowl. Set aside.

9. Whisk together the powdered sugar, corn syrup, vanilla, and 3 tablespoons of heavy cream in a small bowl until smooth. If the mixture is too thick, add 1 additional teaspoon of heavy cream at a time until the desired consistency is reached.

10. Pour half of the icing into a separate small bowl. Stir in the espresso mixture until it's homogenous. Transfer both icings to separate piping bags, both fitted with flat tips.

To assemble:

11. Whisk the chilled mocha crème pâtissière until smooth, then transfer it to a piping bag fitted with a filling tip. Insert the tip into one end of the éclair and pipe the filling in until you can just feel the éclair begin to expand. Be careful not to overfill, or the éclairs may split—work slowly and carefully. If necessary, insert the tip into the opposite end to finish filling the éclair.

12. Repeat this process until all the éclairs are filled. Pipe the vanilla icing over the éclairs, then pipe three zigzag stripes across the width of each éclair with the espresso icing. Let the icing set for 20 to 30 minutes (if you can wait that long) before serving. Keep chilled and serve cold.

note: If your icing has a thin enough consistency, you can also drag a toothpick along the length of the éclairs while the icing is still wet, moving in the direction of the zigzag points, to create a more feathered pattern.

Taillow
Chocolate Cherry Olive Oil Cake

Taillow are small but mighty and undaunted. It's easy for flavors to get lost in chocolate cakes, but the cherries in this olive oil cake hold their own against the dark chocolate. Instead of rolling over and getting overwhelmed by chocolatey goodness, they stand out, like a courageous and defiant Taillow, adding bursts of tart flavor and rich red color throughout the cake.

Difficulty: ● ○ ○ ○
Prep time: 15 minutes
Bake time: 50 minutes
Yield: Serves 12 to 16
Dietary notes: Vegetarian

Equipment: 8-inch round cake pan, stand mixer, wire cooling rack, microwave

½ cup olive oil

½ cup tart cherry juice

¾ cup lightly packed brown sugar

½ teaspoon kosher salt

4 ounces dark chocolate, melted and cooled

2 large eggs

1 tablespoon vanilla extract

1 teaspoon almond extract

1 cup all-purpose flour

½ cup cocoa powder

½ teaspoon baking soda

1 cup dried cherries

Dark chocolate

White chocolate

Red candy melts

1. Preheat the oven to 325°F. Grease an 8-inch cake pan and line the bottom with a circle of parchment paper. Grease the parchment paper.

2. Beat the olive oil, cherry juice, brown sugar, and salt together in a stand mixer fitted with a paddle attachment until combined. Add the chocolate and mix to combine. Add the eggs, one at a time, beating until fully incorporated before adding the next egg. Mix in the vanilla and almond extracts.

3. Mixing on low, add the flour, cocoa powder, and baking soda, mixing until just combined. Fold in the dried cherries. Pour the batter into the prepared cake pan and bake for 45 to 50 minutes or until a cake tester inserted into the center of the cake comes out with just a few moist crumbs on it.

4. Let the cake cool in the pan for 15 minutes before turning it out and flipping it onto a wire rack to cool completely.

5. Add the dark chocolate to a microwave-safe bowl and microwave in 30-second bursts, stirring each time, until the chocolate is melted and smooth. Repeat this process with the white chocolate and red candy melts.

6. Drizzle the dark chocolate, white chocolate, and red candy melts all over the cooled cake. Cut and serve at room temperature.

Whismur
Lemon-Lavender Bars

Whismur may look cute, quiet, and unassuming, but it can let out an ear-splitting scream at a moment's notice. Likewise, these lemon-lavender bars look sweet and simple with a cute lavender icing on top, but that lemon hiding underneath might make you pucker!

Difficulty: ● ● ○ ○
Prep time: 30 minutes
Bake time: 1 hour
Rest time: 1½ hours
Chill time: 1 hour
Yield: 24 bars
Dietary notes: Vegetarian

Equipment: 9-by-13-inch baking pan, food processor, medium saucier, small saucepan, offset spatula

Crust

1 cup all-purpose flour

½ cup powdered sugar

½ teaspoon kosher salt

1½ teaspoons culinary lavender

8 tablespoons unsalted butter, cubed

Lemon Curd

1½ cups sugar

1 tablespoon cornstarch

1 cup lemon juice

3 large eggs

4 large egg yolks

4 tablespoons unsalted butter

Lavender Icing

3 tablespoons whole milk

2 teaspoons culinary lavender

1 drop red food coloring (optional)

3 to 4 drops blue food coloring (optional)

1 cup powdered sugar

Black gel icing

To make the crust:

1. Preheat the oven to 325°F. Grease a 9-by-13-inch baking pan, then line it with parchment paper so that there is a 2-inch overhang of parchment on the long edges.

2. Add the flour, powdered sugar, salt, lavender, and butter to the bowl of a food processor. Pulse until combined and the mixture resembles wet sand.

3. Press the crust into the bottom of the prepared pan and up the sides by about ½ inch. Use the flat bottom of a drinking glass or measuring cup to really compress the crust. Bake for 30 minutes until the crust is just beginning to turn golden. Remove from the oven and set aside.

To make the lemon curd:

4. Whisk together the sugar and cornstarch in a medium saucier to combine, then add the lemon juice, eggs, and egg yolks, whisking to combine. Place the saucier over medium heat and continue whisking gently and constantly until the mixture comes to a boil, about 5 to 7 minutes. Once it starts boiling, continue cooking and whisking for about 30 seconds before removing it from the heat. Stir in the butter until it's melted and smooth.

note: Sauciers have curved bottoms, which makes them preferable when a mixture will likely get trapped in the edges of a straight-sided saucepan. A saucepan is okay to use if you don't have a saucier, but you'll have to be extra vigilant and thorough with stirring so that the mixture doesn't get trapped in the edges and burn.

5. Pour the lemon curd onto the prepared crust, then return the pan to a 325°F oven and bake for an additional 15 to 20 minutes until the filling is set. Remove the pan from the oven and let cool for 1 hour before moving it to the fridge to chill completely.

continued on the next page

To make the lavender icing:

6. Make the icing as the lemon bars cool. Bring the milk and lavender to a boil in a small saucepan over high heat. Remove from heat, cover, and let sit for at least 30 minutes. Strain into a bowl and discard the lavender.

7. Place the powdered sugar in a medium bowl. Stir the lavender-infused milk together with the food coloring (if using), then stir it into the powdered sugar until smooth. Pour the icing over the chilled lemon bars, spreading in an even layer with an offset spatula. Let the bars set, uncovered, in the fridge for 1 hour.

8. Use the overhanging parchment paper to carefully lift the lemon bars out of the baking pan and transfer them to a cutting board. Use a sharp knife to cut them into 24 bars. Decorate each bar with 2 "+" symbols made up of four dots using black gel icing. Keep chilled and serve cold.

note: Creating a sling with parchment paper or aluminum foil is always a good idea. It makes removing your bakes from their vessels much easier and can help prevent breakage.

Spoink
Black Sesame Cream Puffs

The pink pearl on Spoink's head amplifies its psychokinetic powers. The cherry on top of this sesame custard–filled cream puff adds a splash of color and bright tartness to these sweet treats, and that's almost as good! Although the sesame paste used in this recipe is deep, dark black, it turns a soft gray, just like Spoink, when mixed into the custard filling.

Difficulty: ● ● ● ○
Prep time: 20 minutes
Bake time: 30 minutes
Rest time: 50 minutes
Chill time: 4 hours
Yield: 12 cream puffs
Dietary notes: Vegetarian

Equipment: Medium saucepan, fine mesh strainer, medium saucier, instant-read thermometer, stand mixer, half-sheet pan, 2 piping bags with large and ½-inch round tips, wire cooling rack

Black Sesame Crème Pâtissière

1½ cups whole milk

½ cup heavy cream

½ cup sugar

3 tablespoons cornstarch

4 large egg yolks

2 tablespoons black sesame paste

Choux Pastry

1 cup whole milk

6 tablespoons unsalted butter

1 tablespoon sugar

¾ teaspoon kosher salt

1 cup all-purpose flour, sifted

4 large eggs

Topping

12 fresh maraschino cherries

To make the black sesame crème pâtissière:

1. Bring the milk and heavy cream to a bare simmer in a medium saucepan over medium heat, stirring occasionally. Remove from heat.

2. Whisk together the sugar and cornstarch. Add the egg yolks and whisk until smooth. While whisking constantly, slowly pour the hot milk and cream mixture into the cornstarch mixture.

3. Pour this mixture back into the saucepan and return it to medium heat. Whisk constantly until the mixture begins to bubble. The moment you see it bubble, set a 1-minute timer and continue to whisk constantly. Remove from heat.

4. Add the black sesame paste to a medium bowl, then set a fine mesh strainer over the bowl. Pour the crème pâtissière through the fine mesh strainer, pushing it through with a rubber spatula. Let it sit for 3 to 5 minutes to allow the black sesame paste to soften, then stir until smooth. Let the crème pâtissière cool for 20 minutes at room temperature before covering and chilling for at least 4 hours.

note: Sauciers have curved bottoms, which makes them preferable when a mixture will likely get trapped in the edges of a straight-sided saucepan. A saucepan is okay to use if you don't have a saucier, but you'll have to be extra vigilant and thorough with stirring so that the mixture doesn't get trapped in the edges and burn.

To make the choux pastry:

5. While the crème pâtissière chills, make the cream puff shells. Bring the milk, butter, sugar, and salt to a boil in a medium saucier over high heat. Remove from heat and vigorously stir in the flour with a wooden spoon until smooth.

6. Return the saucier to high heat and continue stirring vigorously until an instant-read thermometer registers 170°F when inserted into the mixture.

continued on the next page

7. Dump the mixture into the bowl of a stand mixer fitted with a paddle attachment. Beat on medium speed until the temperature drops to 145°F or lower. Start taking the temperature after about 3 minutes, then continue beating for 1 minute at a time until the correct temperature is reached.

8. Add the eggs one at a time, beating at medium speed until fully incorporated before adding the next egg. Once all the eggs are in, stop the mixer, scrape down the sides, and beat on medium speed for another 5 to 10 seconds until fully mixed.

9. Preheat the oven to 400°F, and line a half-sheet pan with parchment.

10. Transfer the choux batter to a large piping bag fitted with a large round tip. To keep the parchment from moving as you work, pipe a small blob of choux pastry under all four corners of the parchment.

11. Pipe 12 equal mounds onto the parchment. Use a wet finger to smooth the tops of each mound. Bake for 30 minutes, until the mounds are a deep golden brown and well puffed. Turn off the oven and prop open the door with a wooden spoon, allowing the cream puffs to sit for another 30 minutes in the warm oven. Transfer them to a wire rack to cool completely.

To assemble:

12. Whisk the chilled black sesame crème pâtissière until smooth, then transfer it to a piping bag fitted with a round tip. Use a serrated knife to carefully saw off the tops of the cream puffs to reveal a 1-inch hole. Pipe the black sesame crème pâtissière into the cream puff, filling the entire pastry; continue piping until a rounded mound stands about 1 inch over the top of the cream puff.

13. Repeat this process until all the cream puffs are filled. Top each one with a maraschino cherry.

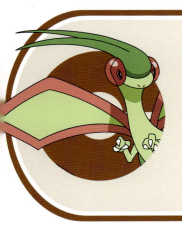

Flygon
Pan Pizza

Flygon love hunting for food with friends, specifically Krookodile. Whip up a batch of this pizza, and you and your friends won't have to hunt for food. Flygon's wings are so powerful that they can create sandstorms—here, we cut the basil into wing shapes to deliver powerful herb-y flavor. With the bursts of red and green from the sauce and basil, and with the olives adding a pleasant earthy note for this Ground-type Pokémon, you might burst into song when you try it, just like the music-like sound you hear when Flygon, the Desert Spirit, flaps its wings.

Difficulty: ● ● ○ ○
Prep time: 20 minutes
Rest time: 2 hours
Bake time: 15 minutes
Yield: 8 slices
Dietary notes: Vegetarian

Equipment: Stand mixer, 12- or 10-inch cast-iron pan

2½ cups bread flour

1½ teaspoons kosher salt

2 teaspoons instant yeast

3 tablespoons olive oil, plus more for the pan

¾ cup lukewarm water

½ cup marinara sauce

8 ounces shredded mozzarella

Kalamata olives

Fresh basil

1. Add the bread flour, salt, yeast, and olive oil to the bowl of a stand mixer fitted with a dough hook attachment. Mix on low to combine, then slowly drizzle in the water. Once a shaggy dough forms (the dough will be lumpy, with no dry flour remaining), increase the speed to medium and knead for 10 to 15 minutes until the dough is smooth and elastic.

2. Pour 2 to 3 tablespoons olive oil into a 12-inch cast-iron pan, tilting the pan to coat the sides and bottom of the pan. You can also use a 10-inch pan, but the dough will be thicker and require more baking time.

3. Transfer the dough to the pan, stretching and pressing the dough toward the edges of the pan. Don't force the dough: Just get it as flat and wide as you can without tearing it—the dough will relax and spread as it rises. Cover the dough and let it rise until it's puffy and has doubled in volume, about 2 hours.

4. For the last 30 minutes of rising time, move one of your oven racks to the lowest position, then preheat the oven to 500°F.

5. Gently stretch the risen dough to the edges of the pan, taking care not to deflate it too much. Spoon the marinara sauce over the top of the dough, spreading it all the way to the edges in an even layer.

6. Scatter the shredded mozzarella over the top of the pizza, all the way to the edges. Top with halved kalamata olives. Bake for 15 minutes or until the top is golden and bubbling. Carefully lift one of the edges of the pizza with a thin metal spatula to check the bottom—it should be golden brown. If it's not golden brown but the top is done, heat the skillet on the stovetop over a medium flame until the crust is the right color.

7. Trim the basil leaves into kite shapes (like Flygon's wings!). Scatter over the top of the hot pizza, slice it into 8 equal wedges, and serve.

Sinnoh Region

Bidoof Peanut Butter
Pretzel Tart

Combee Honey Cake

Kricketot Chocolate
Strawberry Sandwich Cookies

Drifloon Blackberry Galette

Gastrodon Cheesecake Swirl
Bars with Chocolate Streusel

Buizel Apricot
Thumbprint Cookies

Bidoof
Peanut Butter Pretzel Tart

Bidoof will gnaw on just about anything, from logs and rocks to people's houses. This peanut butter tart won't help a Bidoof hone its big front teeth, but it tastes an awful lot better than rocks and logs. The malty, salty pretzel crust pairs beautifully with the sweetened peanut butter filling and rich chocolate ganache, creating a rich tart and a crunchy, satisfying tribute to the imperturbable Plump Mouse Pokémon.

Difficulty: ●●○○
Prep time: 20 minutes
Bake time: 15 minutes
Chill time: 4 hours
Yield: Serves 8 to 12
Dietary notes: Vegetarian

Equipment: Food processor, 9-inch tart pan with removable bottom, wire cooling rack, stand mixer, hand mixer, offset spatula, three piping bags (one with large round tip and one with fine writing tip), microwave

Crust

2 cups pretzels

3 tablespoons packed light brown sugar

6 tablespoons unsalted butter, melted

Filling

8 ounces cream cheese

¼ cup lightly packed light brown sugar

1 cup smooth peanut butter

1 cup powdered sugar

1 cup heavy cream, plus 3 tablespoons for assembling

Decorations

3 ounces dark chocolate, chopped

1 ounce white chocolate

1 maraschino cherry

To make the crust:

1. Preheat the oven to 350°F. Add the pretzels and brown sugar to the bowl of a food processor. Pulse until finely ground. Transfer to a medium bowl.

2. Stir the butter into the pretzel mixture until fully incorporated. Press the mixture into the bottom and all the way up the sides of a 9-inch tart pan with a removable bottom. Use the smooth bottom of a drinking glass or measuring cup to fully compact the crust.

3. Bake the crust for 15 minutes until slightly darkened and set. Allow to cool completely on a wire cooling rack.

To make the filling:

4. Beat the cream cheese, brown sugar, and peanut butter in the bowl of a stand mixer fitted with a paddle attachment at medium speed until light, fluffy, and smooth. Reduce the speed to low, then add the powdered sugar. Beat until combined, then increase the speed to medium-high, beating until light, fluffy, and smooth, about 8 to 10 minutes.

5. Add 1 cup of the heavy cream to a large bowl. Beat with a handheld mixer until soft peaks form, about 5 minutes. Carefully fold the whipped cream into the peanut butter mixture.

6. Spoon the mixture into the cooled tart shell, smoothing and leveling the filling with an offset spatula. Reserve about 1 cup of the filling.

7. Spoon the remaining filling into a piping bag fitted with a large round tip. Pipe the filling into puffy swoops all along the outer edge of the tart, just like Bidoof's fluffy cheeks.

8. Add the dark chocolate and 3 tablespoons of heavy cream to a small bowl. Microwave for 1 minute and stir until smooth. If solid bits of chocolate remain, microwave for an additional 15 seconds at a time until fully melted and smooth. Let the ganache cool slightly.

continued on the next page

9. As the ganache cools, add the white chocolate to a microwave-safe bowl and microwave in bursts of 30 seconds, stirring each time, until melted and smooth. Transfer the white chocolate to a small piping bag and snip off the end.

To decorate:

10. Transfer the chocolate ganache to a piping bag fitted with a fine writing tip. Pipe an outline of Bidoof's eyes and muzzle. Pipe a large square of white chocolate in the lower center of the muzzle to form Bidoof's teeth.

11. Fill in the muzzle with the chocolate ganache. Pipe two small dots for Bidoof's eyes. After a few minutes, if the eyes are set, pipe two smaller white dots on top to finish the eyes. (If the ganache isn't set, chill for 5 to 10 minutes before piping the white chocolate on.) Pipe a thin outline around the teeth, plus one line straight up the middle to separate them into two teeth. Drizzle any remaining ganache in decorative swirls all over the fluffy mounds of filling you piped earlier. Halve the maraschino cherry, and place one half in the center of the muzzle to form Bidoof's nose. (Feel free to snack on the other half of the cherry!) The filling should be cold enough to set the ganache as you work—if not, chill for 20 additional minutes before slicing and serving.

Combee
Honey Cake

Combee are one of the hardest-working Pokémon, spending their days gathering nectar. Both this cake and its frosting are just as sweet as the nectar Combee collects, and when you share this delicate honey cake with dear friends, you'll feel as close as the hundreds of Combee who sleep packed together in a drowsy, satisfied clump.

Difficulty: ● ○ ○ ○
Prep time: 15 minutes
Bake time: 50 minutes
Yield: Serves 8 to 12
Dietary notes: Vegetarian

Equipment: 8-inch cake pan, stand mixer, wire cooling rack, hand mixer, offset spatula, microwave, piping bags with flat nozzle and fine writing tip

Cake

8 tablespoons unsalted butter, room temperature

½ cup sugar

½ cup honey

2 large eggs

1 teaspoon vanilla extract

½ cup whole milk

1⅔ cups all-purpose flour

1¼ teaspoons baking powder

½ teaspoon baking soda

½ teaspoon kosher salt

Frosting

6 tablespoons unsalted butter

⅓ cup honey

2 cups powdered sugar

¼ teaspoon kosher salt

1 tablespoon lemon juice

Red food coloring

Yellow food coloring

Decorations

¼ cup dark chocolate chips

To make the cake:

1. Preheat the oven to 350°F. Grease an 8-inch cake pan and line the bottom with a circle of parchment paper. Grease the parchment paper.

2. Add the butter, sugar, and honey to the bowl of a stand mixer fitted with a paddle attachment. Cream together at medium speed until light and fluffy, about 5 to 7 minutes. Beat in the eggs, one at a time, allowing each egg to fully incorporate.

3. Beat in the vanilla and milk. Reduce the mixer speed to low, then add the flour, baking powder, baking soda, and salt, mixing until just incorporated. Scrape down the sides and bottom of the bowl with a rubber spatula to ensure that the batter is homogenous.

4. Scrape the batter into the prepared pan, smoothing the top with a rubber spatula. Bake for 45 to 50 minutes, until a cake tester or toothpick inserted into the center of the cake comes out with just a few moist crumbs. Let the cake cool in the pan for 20 minutes before transferring it to a wire rack to cool completely.

To make the frosting:

5. Using a handheld mixer, beat together the butter, honey, powdered sugar, salt, and lemon juice in a large bowl until smooth, about 8 to 10 minutes.

6. Remove ⅓ cup of frosting and transfer to a clean small bowl. Add 1 to 2 drops of red food coloring and 4 to 6 drops of yellow food coloring to make orange frosting. Beat until uniform in color, about 1 minute. Remove 1 teaspoon of the original, uncolored frosting and transfer to a small bowl. Add 4 to 6 drops of red food coloring and stir with a spoon until uniform in color to make red frosting. (If you want your uncolored base frosting to be yellower, add a few drops of yellow food coloring until it matches Combee.)

continued on the next page

To decorate:

7. If the cake is quite domed, trim off the rounded top of the cake with a serrated knife to level it. Draw a Combee template of all three Combee hexagons together on an 8-inch round of parchment paper—the Combee will be about 7 inches wide at its widest and 7 inches tall from the top of the upper hexagon to the bottom of the lower hexagon. Cut the template out and place it on top of the cake. Use a sharp knife to cut the cake into Combee's shape using the template as your guide. (Snack on the trimmings while you decorate!)

8. Spread the yellow base frosting evenly over the top and sides of the cake with an offset spatula. Add the orange frosting to a small piping bag fitted with a flat nozzle. Pipe the frosting into three hexagonal shapes to create the outline around the faces on Combee. Dip your finger in water and use it to smooth out any rough spots or overlaps. Use a small offset spatula to create the small red wedge shape on the lower face, or pipe it with another flat nozzle and smooth it with the spatula or your finger.

9. Heat the chocolate chips in a microwave-safe bowl on high for 30-second bursts, stirring each time, until melted and smooth. Let cool slightly, then transfer to a piping bag with a fine writing tip. Pipe two eyes and a smiling mouth onto each of the three faces. Pipe two antennae (about 2 to 3 inches long) onto a quarter-sheet pan lined with parchment paper. Chill until completely set, about 10 to 15 minutes, then insert into the top corner of the top two faces.

> **note:** Unable to make a template? Try these steps with your round cake: Cut a short but wide "v" out of the top of the cake. From each side of the "v," cut down horizontally toward the sides of the cake at a similar angle. Cut straight down, then cut horizontally down into the cake, at the same angle as the cut above. Cut straight down from there, then cut horizontally down toward the bottom of the cake to create the bottom point. Repeat on the other side of the cake, mirroring your work as much as possible. Aim for each edge being as straight and equal in length to all the other sides.

Kricketot
Chocolate Strawberry Sandwich Cookies

Kricketot are musical in nature—they make xylophone sounds by clanging their antennae together—so we recommend using cookie cutters shaped like music notes to make these sandwich cookies. Of course, they'll be tasty no matter what, and the cookies and filling are similar to Kricketot's coloring, so use whatever shape you have on hand.

Difficulty: ●○○○
Prep time: 15 minutes
Chill time: 1 hour
Bake time: 14 minutes
Yield: About 12 sandwich cookies
Dietary notes: Vegetarian

Equipment: Food processor, sheet pan, half-sheet pan, wire cooling rack

1¼ cups all-purpose flour
⅓ cup cocoa powder
8 tablespoons unsalted butter, softened
½ cup sugar
½ teaspoon kosher salt
1 large egg
Strawberry jam

1. Add the flour, cocoa powder, butter, sugar, and salt to the bowl of a food processor. Pulse until combined. Add the egg and pulse until a soft dough forms.

2. Sandwich the dough between two sheets of parchment paper. Roll out to a thickness of ⅛ inch. Transfer to a sheet pan, then freeze for 1 hour.

3. Preheat the oven to 350°F.

4. Remove the top layer of parchment from the cookie dough. Punch out as many cookies in your chosen shape as you can. Gather up the scraps, sandwich them between the two sheets of parchment, roll out the dough, and punch out more cookies, repeating the process until you can no longer make more cookies.

5. Transfer the cookies to a parchment-lined half-sheet pan. Leave about ½ inch between the cookies—they won't spread very much, if at all.

6. Bake the cookies for 12 to 14 minutes, or until set. Let cool for 5 minutes on the pan, then transfer them to a wire rack to cool completely.

7. Spread a thin layer of strawberry jam onto the flat side of a cookie, then sandwich with a second cookie. Repeat until you've used up all the cookies.

Drifloon
Blackberry Galette

Eek! Did you know that sometimes when children hang onto a Drifloon, they disappear? Well, after taking just one bite of this blackberry galette, the only thing at risk of disappearing is the rest of the galette. Packed with luscious blackberries, the filling in this galette is a deep purple, reminiscent of Drifloon, and the whipped cream looks just like the fluff on Drifloon's head!

Difficulty: ● ● ○ ○
Prep time: 20 minutes
Chill time: 1 hour
Bake time: 35 minutes
Yield: Serves 8
Dietary notes: Vegetarian

Equipment: Food processor, half-sheet pan, wire cooling rack, hand mixer

Crust

1 cup all-purpose flour

½ cup rye flour

8 tablespoons unsalted butter, cubed

½ teaspoon kosher salt

1 tablespoon sugar

1 large egg

2 tablespoons heavy cream

Filling

18 ounces blackberries

¾ cup sugar

Zest and juice of 1 lemon

3 tablespoons cornstarch

To Assemble and Serve

1 large egg

Yellow decorative sugar

Raw sugar

1 cup heavy cream

2 tablespoons powdered sugar

note: Rye flour adds a nutty flavor and a crunchier texture to the galette crust, but you can substitute additional all-purpose flour if rye flour is unavailable.

1. Add the flour, rye flour, butter, salt, and sugar to the bowl of a food processor. Pulse until the mixture resembles wet sand. Add 1 egg and 2 tablespoons heavy cream and process until the dough forms. Shape into a disc, wrap tightly in plastic, and chill for 1 hour.

2. For the filling, combine the blackberries, sugar, lemon zest and juice, and cornstarch in a large bowl. Toss to evenly coat.

3. Preheat the oven to 400°F. Line a half-sheet pan with parchment.

4. Place the chilled dough onto a floured work surface. Remove about 2 tablespoons of dough and set aside. Roll out the remaining dough to a thickness of about ¼ inch, then transfer it to the prepared sheet pan.

5. To assemble, spoon the filling into the center of the crust, leaving a border of about 2 inches. Fold the edges of the crust toward the center, pleating every few inches or so.

6. Shape the 2 tablespoons of dough you set aside into a + shape at an angle. Place on the same pan as the galette.

7. Beat the egg together with 1 tablespoon water. Brush the crust of the galette and the + with the egg wash. Coat the + shape in yellow sugar and sprinkle raw sugar on the crust of the galette.

8. Transfer the sheet pan to the oven, and bake for 35 minutes. About 10 to 12 minutes into the cook time, remove the + with a spatula and transfer it to a wire rack to cool.

9. Let the galette cool directly on the pan. Place the + at an angle on the exposed fruit in the center of the cooled galette.

10. To serve, beat the heavy cream and powdered sugar in a medium bowl with a handheld mixer on medium until medium peaks form. Slice and serve the galette with three-lobed dollops of whipped cream that look like the fluff on Drifloon's head.

Gastrodon
Cheesecake Swirl Bars with Chocolate Streusel

Gastrodon's body can be blue or pink, depending on whether it comes from the western side or eastern side of Sinnoh, respectively. With this cheesecake bar recipe, you can choose a raspberry swirl for an East Sea look, or a blueberry swirl for a West Sea look. The crispy streusel topping evokes Gastrodon's plate, a remnant from the huge protective shell it had in ancient times.

Difficulty: ● ● ○ ○
Prep time: 20 minutes
Bake time: 1 hour
Chill time: 4 hours
Yield: 24 bars
Dietary notes: Vegetarian

Equipment: 9-by-13-inch baking pan, food processor, hand mixer, medium saucepan, blender, fine mesh strainer

Crust
16 ounces graham crackers (10 to 12 crackers)
2 tablespoons packed light brown sugar
½ teaspoon kosher salt
4 tablespoons unsalted butter, melted

Filling
Three 8-ounce packages cream cheese, softened
½ cup sour cream, room temperature
1 cup sugar
1 tablespoon vanilla paste or extract
3 large eggs, room temperature

Fruit Swirl
12 ounces frozen raspberries or blueberries
¼ cup sugar
Zest and juice of 1 lemon

Chocolate Streusel Topping
¾ cup all-purpose flour
⅓ cup cocoa powder
¼ cup lightly packed light brown sugar
¼ teaspoon kosher salt
5 tablespoons butter, melted

To make the crust:

1. Preheat the oven to 350°F. Grease a 9-by-13-inch baking pan, then line the pan with parchment paper so there is a 2-inch overhang on the long sides of the pan.

2. Add the graham crackers, brown sugar, and salt to the bowl of a food processor. Pulse until finely ground. Tip the contents into a large bowl, then pour in the butter. Stir until no dry crumbs remain.

3. Press the crust mixture into the bottom of the prepared pan, using the flat bottom of a drinking glass or measuring cup to tightly pack the crust. Bake for about 20 minutes, until the crust is set and just beginning to darken. Set aside and let cool while you make the filling.

To make the filling:

4. Add the cream cheese, sour cream, and sugar to a large bowl. Beat together with a handheld mixer until light and fluffy. Add the vanilla and mix to combine. Add the eggs one at a time, beating until each egg is fully incorporated before adding the next one.

5. Pour the filling onto the prepared crust and set aside while you make the fruit swirl.

note: You can instead use 6 ounces of frozen raspberries and 6 ounces of frozen blueberries to create a real West Sea and East Sea experience. Combine each type of berry with half the sugar and half the lemon juice and zest, following the purée instructions in step 6 one at a time, then spoon each purée over half of the filling and carefully swirl each half without intermixing them in step 8. To be true to nature, serve the blueberry bars on the left for the West Sea and the raspberry bars on the right for the East Sea!

To make the fruit swirl:

6. Add the berries, sugar, and lemon zest and juice to a medium saucepan. Cook over medium heat, stirring occasionally, until the berries begin to break down, release their juices, and start to bubble. Let cool, then transfer the berries to a blender. Blend until smooth, then pour the fruit purée through a fine mesh strainer into a bowl. Discard the solids, and let the strained purée cool while you make the streusel topping.

To make the chocolate streusel topping and finish:

7. Whisk together the flour, cocoa powder, brown sugar, and salt in a small bowl until combined. Stir in the butter until a wet, crumbly mixture forms.

8. Spoon the fruit purée over the cheesecake filling. Gently swirl a butter knife through the cheesecake filling to create a marbled effect, but be careful not to overmix. Sprinkle the streusel topping over the top of the cheesecake.

9. Bake for 35 to 40 minutes until set. The cheesecake will be a bit wobbly in the center, but it shouldn't be totally liquid. Let cool at room temperature for 1 hour, then move to the fridge to chill for at least 4 hours. Cut into 24 squares, then serve.

Buizel
Apricot Thumbprint Cookies

These cookies emulate the shape of Buizel's collar, which it uses as a floatation device, with an orange-colored, apricot-flavored center. We tame the sweetness of the cookie and filling with some dark chocolate whiskers that give each cookie extra depth—and, of course, cuteness.

Difficulty: ● ○ ○ ○
Prep time: 15 minutes
Bake time: 15 minutes
Yield: 18 cookies
Dietary notes: Vegetarian

Equipment: 2 half-sheet pans, hand mixer, wire cooling racks, microwave, piping bag with fine writing tip

1½ cups all-purpose flour

½ cup almond flour

10 tablespoons unsalted butter, softened

⅔ cup sugar

1 large egg

2 teaspoons vanilla extract

½ teaspoon almond extract

¼ cup apricot jam

Dark chocolate, chopped

1. Preheat the oven to 350°F. Line two half-sheet pans with parchment paper.

2. Whisk together the flour and almond flour in a large bowl. Add the butter and sugar, then beat together with a handheld mixer until combined. Beat in the egg, followed by the vanilla and almond extracts.

3. Scoop 9 walnut-size balls of cookie dough onto one of the prepared sheet pans. Repeat with the remaining dough and sheet pan. Use your thumb to make a divot in each cookie. Spoon about ½ teaspoon of jam into each divot.

4. Bake for about 15 minutes, until the cookies are set and just turning golden brown around the edges. Cool in the pan for 10 minutes before transferring the cookies to a wire rack to cool completely.

5. When the cookies are cool, add the chopped dark chocolate to a microwave-safe bowl. Microwave in 30-second bursts, stirring each time, until the chocolate is melted and smooth. Spoon into a small piping bag fitted with a fine writing tip.

6. Pipe a nose in the center of the jam, then pipe two sets of whiskers on opposite sides of each cookie to match Buizel's face.

Unova Region

Snivy Lemon Biscotti with Chocolate, Pistachios & Candied Lemon Peel

Tepig Spiced Chocolate Bundt Cake

Oshawott Blueberry Meringue Tartlets

Sandile Butterscotch & Brownie Parfait

Scraggy Orange Cardamom Sweet Rolls

Whimsicott Angel Food Cake

Snivy
Lemon Biscotti with Chocolate, Pistachios & Candied Lemon Peel

Snivy uses its tail to get energy from sunlight, but humans get energy from rest and, of course, food! This crunchy biscotti is packed with bright lemony flavor, so every bite tastes a little like sunshine (and pistachios and chocolate!). Even the most discerning Snivy would approve. Serve with coffee or tea of your choice for a calming afternoon snack—and stretch out in the sun for the fully Snivy experience.

Difficulty: ● ● ● ○
Prep time: 15 minutes
Bake time: 55 minutes
Yield: About 30 biscotti
Dietary notes: Vegetarian

Equipment: Half-sheet pan, stand mixer, wire cooling rack

8 tablespoons unsalted butter, softened
⅓ cup sugar
⅓ cup packed light brown sugar
½ teaspoon kosher salt
1 tablespoon lemon zest
3 large eggs, divided
1 tablespoon vanilla
2 cups all-purpose flour
2 teaspoons baking powder
½ cup chopped pistachios
½ cup dark chocolate chips
½ cup chopped candied lemon peel
Raw sugar

1. Preheat the oven to 350°F. Line a half-sheet pan with parchment paper.

2. Beat together the butter, sugar, brown sugar, salt, and lemon zest in the bowl of a stand mixer fitted with a paddle attachment until light and fluffy, about 5 minutes. Beat in 2 eggs, along with the vanilla, on medium speed until fully incorporated, about 2 to 3 minutes.

3. Reduce the mixer speed to low, then add the flour and baking powder. Mix until just about incorporated, then add the pistachios, chocolate chips, and candied peel, mixing until evenly distributed.

4. Shape the dough into a flat, thick sheet that's about 15 inches long, 6 inches wide, and 1 inch tall. Place the dough on the prepared sheet pan. Beat the remaining egg together with 1 tablespoon water. Brush the top of the log with a thin coating of egg wash, then sprinkle liberally with raw sugar.

5. Bake the log for 30 to 35 minutes, until firm, and light golden brown. Let the biscotti log cool until you're able to handle it safely (note that it should still be warm, but not hot). Transfer to a cutting board, and carefully cut ½-inch slices crosswise from the log with a serrated knife, for a total of about 30 biscotti.

6. Transfer the cut biscotti back to the prepared sheet pan, cut side up. They will not spread, so don't worry about leaving a ton of room between each one—½ inch will do. Reduce the oven temperature to 325°F and bake for about 10 minutes, or until lightly browned.

7. Carefully flip over the biscotti, then bake for an additional 10 minutes, or until lightly browned. Let the biscotti cool on the pan for 5 minutes, then transfer them to a wire rack to cool completely.

Tepig
Spiced Chocolate Bundt Cake

This delicious chocolate cake gets a fiery kick from chili powder mixed into the batter, as well as some warm aromatic cinnamon. When it comes time to bake, stick with your trusty oven and don't depend on Tepig's fireballs. The cake is topped with spicy red cinnamon candies shaped like the ball on Tepig's tail.

Difficulty: ● ● ○ ○
Prep time: 20 minutes
Bake time: 50 minutes
Yield: Serves 12 to 16
Dietary notes: Vegetarian

Equipment: 9-inch Bundt pan, stand mixer, wire cooling rack

Cake
1 cup cocoa powder

2 teaspoons instant espresso powder

1 cup boiling water

1 cup buttermilk

1 cup unsalted butter, melted

1 cup sugar

1 cup packed dark brown sugar

Zest of 1 orange

1 tablespoon vanilla extract

3 eggs, room temperature

3 cups all-purpose flour

1 teaspoon baking powder

½ teaspoon baking soda

1 teaspoon kosher salt

2 teaspoons ancho chile powder

1 teaspoon cinnamon

¼ teaspoon cayenne

Icing
1 cup powdered sugar

Zest of 1 orange

2 tablespoons orange juice

1 tablespoon heavy cream

1 drop red food coloring (optional)

6 to 8 drops yellow food coloring (optional)

⅓ cup small cinnamon candies, or to taste

1. Preheat the oven to 350°F. Grease a 9-inch Bundt pan.

2. Whisk together the cocoa powder, instant espresso powder, and boiling water. Let sit for 2 minutes, then pour the liquid into the bowl of a stand mixer fitted with a paddle attachment. Add the buttermilk, butter, sugar, dark brown sugar, orange zest, and vanilla. Beat until smooth, about 5 minutes.

3. Add the eggs, one at a time, beating on medium until fully incorporated before adding the next egg.

4. Whisk together the flour, baking powder, baking soda, salt, ancho chile powder, cinnamon, and cayenne in a medium bowl. Reduce the mixer speed to low, and gradually add the flour mixture until it is fully combined. Scrape down the sides and bottom of the bowl to make sure the mixture is homogenous.

5. Pour the batter into the prepared pan, smoothing the top of the batter with a rubber spatula. Bake for 45 to 50 minutes, until a cake tester inserted into the center of the cake comes out clean. Let the cake cool in the pan for 30 minutes, before carefully inverting it onto a wire rack to cool completely.

6. Make the icing by beating together the powdered sugar, orange zest, orange juice, heavy cream, and red and yellow food coloring (if using) in a large bowl until smooth, about 8 to 10 minutes. Drizzle the icing over the top of the cooled cake, then scatter small cinnamon candies over the icing.

Oshawott
Blueberry Meringue Tartlets

Oshawott sometimes uses the scalchop on its stomach to break open hard berries, but there's no need to worry about the berries in this tart. They're soft, juicy, and delicious, especially when topped with light, fluffy meringue and delicious chocolate details that reflect the adorable Sea Otter Pokémon!

Difficulty: ● ● ○ ○
Prep time: 30 minutes
Bake time: 30 minutes
Chill time: 1 hour and 10 minutes
Yield: 12 tartlets
Dietary notes: Vegetarian

Equipment: Food processor, 12-cup muffin tin or 12 fluted tartlet pans, 4-inch cookie cutter, stand mixer or hand mixer, four piping bags (one with large round tip and three with fine writing tips), microwave, half-sheet pan

Tart Shells

1½ cups all-purpose flour

½ teaspoon kosher salt

2 tablespoons sugar

8 tablespoons unsalted butter, cubed

2 to 3 tablespoons cold water

Filling

2 cups blueberries, fresh or frozen

½ cup sugar

1 tablespoon cornstarch

Juice and zest of 1 lemon

To Assemble

12 blueberries

3 large egg whites

½ cup sugar

White chocolate

Dark chocolate

Milk chocolate

To make the tart:

1. Add the flour, salt, sugar, and butter to the bowl of a food processor. Pulse until the mixture resembles coarse sand. Add 2 tablespoons of water, and pulse until a smooth dough forms. If the dough is too dry, add 1 tablespoon of water, and pulse to combine.

2. Shape the dough into a disc, tightly wrap with plastic, and chill for at least 1 hour.

3. Meanwhile, add the blueberries, sugar, cornstarch, lemon zest, and lemon juice to a large bowl. Toss to combine, then lightly mash with a fork to break up some of the blueberries. No need to crush all of them—half or less is fine. Set aside.

4. Heat the oven to 400°F. Grease a standard muffin tin or 12 fluted tartlet pans. Place the chilled dough onto a floured work surface. Roll out to a thickness of about ⅛ inch. Use a 4-inch round cookie cutter to punch out 12 circles of dough. If necessary, gather up and reroll the scraps to punch out additional circles.

5. Press the dough into the prepared muffin tin or tartlet pans. Give the blueberry filling a quick stir to redistribute, then spoon it into the tart shells, dividing evenly.

6. Bake for 25 to 30 minutes, until the tart shells are golden and the filling is bubbling. Let the tartlets cool completely in the pan before removing them, loosening the edges with a thin knife, if necessary.

To make the meringue:

7. Beat the egg whites on medium speed in the bowl of a stand mixer or using a handheld mixer, until thick and foamy. Continue beating while gradually adding the sugar. Increase the speed to medium-high and beat until stiff peaks form. Transfer the meringue to a piping bag fitted with a large round tip.

continued on the next page

To assemble:

8. Pipe a sphere of meringue onto each of the cooled tarts. Smooth the tops of the spheres with a wet finger. Place the blueberries on either side of the meringue to form Oshawott's ears. Chill, uncovered, in the fridge while you prepare the chocolate decorations.

9. Place the white, dark, and milk chocolates into separate microwave-safe bowls. Microwave in bursts of 30 seconds, stirring each time, until all the chocolate is melted and smooth. Transfer the three chocolates into three separate piping bags fitted with fine writing tips.

10. Line a half-sheet pan with parchment. Pipe 24 dark chocolate circles to form Oshawott's eyes. Freeze for about 1 minute to set.

11. Pipe 24 white chocolate dots over the set dark chocolate to complete Oshawott's eyes. Pipe 72 tiny dots in dark chocolate to form the little spots on Oshawott's face, followed by 12 mouth shapes.

12. Pipe 12 milk chocolate spots to form Oshawott's nose. Chill to set for about 5 to 10 minutes.

13. Place 2 eyes, 1 nose, 1 mouth, and 6 spots on each tart to form Oshawott's face. Keep chilled and serve cold.

Sandile
Butterscotch & Brownie Parfait

The layers of this parfait are inspired by Sandile's black and tan stripes. Although Sandile's belly is pink, this dessert features a delicate pink raspberry whipped cream on the top—think of it as a Sandile flipped on its back asking for belly scratches. These parfaits are so tasty, they might just coax a Sandile or two out of their hiding spots deep in the sand.

Difficulty: ● ○ ○ ○
Prep time: 20 minutes
Bake time: 17 minutes
Chill time: 4 hours
Yield: 4 parfaits
Dietary notes: Vegetarian

Equipment: Medium saucepan, fine mesh strainer, half-sheet pan, hand mixer

Butterscotch Crème Pâtissière

1½ cups whole milk

½ cup heavy cream

½ cup sugar

3 tablespoons cornstarch

4 large egg yolks

1 teaspoon vanilla extract

¾ cup butterscotch chips

Crisp Brownie

½ cup sugar

½ cup packed light brown sugar

8 tablespoons unsalted butter, melted

½ cup dark chocolate chips, melted

½ cup black cocoa powder or regular cocoa powder

2 eggs

½ cup all-purpose flour

½ teaspoon kosher salt

Raspberry Whipped Cream

1 cup heavy cream

¼ cup powdered sugar

1 tablespoon raspberry powder, or raspberry purée

1. Bring the milk and heavy cream to a bare simmer in a medium saucepan over medium heat, stirring occasionally. Remove from heat.

2. Whisk together the sugar and cornstarch. Add the egg yolks and whisk until smooth. While whisking constantly, slowly pour the milk and cream mixture into the cornstarch mixture.

3. Pour this mixture back into the saucepan and return to medium heat. Whisk constantly until the mixture begins to bubble. The moment you see it bubble, set a 1-minute timer and continue to whisk constantly. Remove from heat.

4. Add the vanilla and butterscotch chips to a medium bowl, then set a fine mesh strainer over the bowl. Pour the crème pâtissière through the fine mesh strainer, pushing it through with a rubber spatula. Let sit for 3 to 5 minutes to allow the butterscotch chips to melt, then stir until smooth. Let cool for 20 minutes at room temperature before covering and chilling for at least 4 hours.

5. Meanwhile, make the brownies. Preheat the oven to 325°F. Line a half-sheet pan with parchment paper, then grease the parchment and sides of the pan.

6. Using a handheld mixer, beat the sugar, brown sugar, butter, chocolate, and black cocoa together in a large bowl until smooth. Beat in the eggs. Add the flour and salt, stirring together until just combined.

7. Spread the brownie batter across the parchment paper in a thin, even layer. It should just barely fill the pan. Bake for 15 to 17 minutes, until just set.

8. Let the brownies cool completely in the pan.

9. Whisk together the heavy cream, powdered sugar, and raspberry powder in a large bowl until soft peaks form, about 5 minutes.

10. Break apart the brownies using your hands—really get in there and break them into chunks and crumbs. Fill 4 dessert cups with alternating layers of crumbled brownies and butterscotch crème pâtissière before topping with a generous dollop of raspberry whipped cream. Keep chilled and serve cold.

Scraggy
Orange Cardamom Sweet Rolls

Scraggy's hide is rubbery and pliable, kind of like uncooked bread dough! Once these sweet rolls are cooked, though, they're light, soft, and springy enough to bounce back no matter how hard Scraggy headbutts them. The rolls are shaped like Scraggy's head, complete with its signature smile in white chocolate, and the flavors are perfect for this dual-type Pokémon. Cardamom is an intense, smoky spice befitting a Dark-type Pokémon, and it's paired with punchy orange to jazz it up, like Scraggy's Fighting-type spirit!

Difficulty: ● ● ○ ○
Prep time: 20 minutes
Rest time: 2 hours
Bake time: 30 minutes
Yield: 12 rolls
Dietary notes: Vegetarian

Equipment: Stand mixer, 9-by-13-inch baking dish, instant-read thermometer, small saucepan, wire cooling rack, microwave, 2 piping bags with fine writing tips

Rolls

1 cup whole milk, lukewarm

¼ cup honey

2½ teaspoons active dry yeast

2 large eggs

4 cups flour

½ teaspoon ground cardamom

1 teaspoon salt

4 tablespoons unsalted butter, softened

1 cup chopped candied orange peel

Cardamom Syrup

¼ cup sugar

¼ cup water

1 teaspoon ground cardamom

Decorations

Dried papaya

White chocolate

Dark chocolate

1. Stir together the milk, honey, and yeast in the bowl of a stand mixer fitted with a dough hook attachment. Let sit for 5 to 10 minutes, until foamy. (If the mixture doesn't foam, the milk may be too warm. The ideal temperature should be between 100°F and 110°F. If it still isn't foaming, your yeast may be dead, and you'll need to purchase new yeast.)

2. Add the eggs, flour, cardamom, and salt. Mix on low until a shaggy dough forms (the dough will be lumpy, with no dry flour remaining), then increase the speed to medium, mixing until the dough is smooth, about 10 minutes.

3. Add half the butter and continue kneading the dough until fully incorporated. Add the remaining butter and continue mixing for 15 minutes until the dough is smooth, slightly glossy, and elastic.

4. Add the chopped candied orange peel and mix until evenly distributed. Cover the bowl and let the dough rise in a warm place for about 1 hour until it has puffed and doubled in size. While the dough rises, grease a 9-by-13-inch baking dish.

5. Gently punch down the dough to deflate, then turn it out onto a floured surface. Divide the dough into 12 equal portions.

6. Working with one piece of dough at a time, shape into a ball. Place the ball on the work surface and gently cup your hand over the dough ball, with your fingertips on the work surface. Rotate the dough to tighten the surface and shape it into a roll. Repeat with all the dough balls, then place them in the prepared baking dish, spacing them evenly. Lightly cover the balls with greased plastic wrap. Let them rise for about 1 hour, until they're puffed and crowding the pan.

7. Toward the end of the rising time, preheat the oven to 350°F. When the rolls have risen, bake them for 25 to 30 minutes until they're golden brown and an instant-read thermometer registers 195°F when inserted into the center of the rolls.

continued on the next page

8. While the rolls are baking, prepare the cardamom syrup. Add the sugar, water, and cardamom to a small saucepan. Bring to a boil over high heat, stirring occasionally until the sugar is dissolved. Remove from heat.

9. Brush the tops of the rolls with the syrup immediately after removing them from the oven. Let the rolls cool in the pan for 10 minutes before transferring them to a wire rack to cool completely.

10. For the decorations, chop the dried papaya into thin sticks about ¾ inch tall. Insert the papaya into the top of each roll to create the small scale on top of Scraggy's head.

11. Add the white chocolate and dark chocolate to separate microwave-safe bowls. Heat both chocolates in the microwave in 30-second bursts until the chocolate is melted and smooth. Transfer the chocolates to separate piping bags fitted with fine writing tips.

12. Using the white chocolate, pipe 2 large circles on either side of each roll to create the white parts of Scraggy's eyes. Pipe 1 semicircle on the lower middle of each roll between the eyes to create Scraggy's mouth.

13. Pipe an outline around the large circles in dark chocolate. Use the dark chocolate to pipe an oblong circle in the center of the white circles to finish Scraggy's eyes.

14. Pipe an outline around the semicircle using dark chocolate, then pipe two lines of dark chocolate on top of the semicircle to finish Scraggy's teeth. Pipe two small dots above the teeth to form Scraggy's nostrils.

Whimsicott
Angel Food Cake

Mischievous little Whimsicott loves to float around on whirlwinds, and this cake is light and fluffy to match! The delicate sweetness of the angel food cake is perfect for this Grass- and Fairy-type Pokémon and Whimsicott's cottony mane. But the addition of a lime curd creates a tart burst of lime on your tongue, not too unlike one of the surprising pranks Whimsicott loves to pull (like leaving cotton all over the place)! The result is a cake that is sweet, surprising, and bright.

Difficulty: ● ● ○ ○
Prep time: 30 minutes
Bake time: 45 minutes
Cool time: 3 hours
Yield: Serves 10 to 12
Dietary notes: Vegetarian

Equipment: 10-inch tube pan with feet, wire cooling rack, medium saucepan, hand mixer, two piping bags (one with large round tip)

Cake
12 large egg whites

1 tablespoon lime juice

1½ cups sugar

1 tablespoon vanilla extract

1¼ cups cake flour

½ teaspoon kosher salt

Lime Curd
¾ cup sugar

2 teaspoons cornstarch

½ cup lime juice

2 large eggs

2 large egg yolks

2 tablespoons unsalted butter

2 teaspoons matcha powder mixed with 1 tablespoon hot water until smooth

3 to 4 drops green food coloring

6 to 10 drops blue food coloring

Whipped Cream
2 cups heavy whipping cream

¼ cup powdered sugar

To make the cake:

1. Place an oven rack on the lower middle position. Preheat the oven to 325°F.

2. Add the egg whites and lime juice to the bowl of a stand mixer fitted with a whisk attachment. Beat on medium-low until frothy, about 1 minute. Increase the speed to medium-high, then very slowly add the sugar as it mixes. Continue beating until soft peaks form, about 5 minutes. Add the vanilla, beating until just combined.

3. Sift together the cake flour and salt. Add ¼ of the flour mixture to the egg white mixture. Gently fold in with a rubber spatula until fully incorporated. Repeat this process three more times, until all the flour mixture is incorporated.

4. Carefully pour the batter into an ungreased 10-inch tube pan with feet. Spread the batter evenly with a rubber spatula. Bake for 40 to 45 minutes, until a cake tester inserted into the center of the cake comes out clean. Flip the pan cake side down and place it on a wire cooling rack to cool for 3 hours. Loosen the edges of the cake with a thin, sharp knife, then turn it back upside down. Tap the bottom of the pan until the cake releases.

To make the lime curd:

5. While the cake cools, make the lime curd. Whisk together the sugar and cornstarch in a medium saucepan. Add the lime juice, eggs, and egg yolks. Whisk until smooth, add the butter, then place the saucepan over medium-low heat.

6. Cook, whisking gently but continuously, until thickened and beginning to bubble. When the first bubble appears, set a 1-minute timer and continue whisking. Remove from heat when the timer goes off. Add the matcha powder and food coloring, adjusting the levels of blue and green to match the green of Whimsicott's horns if necessary, and whisk until homogenous.

continued on page 87

7. Transfer the lime curd to a bowl, then cover it with plastic wrap, pressing the plastic directly onto the surface of the curd to prevent a skin from forming on top. Chill for 1 hour.

To make the whipped cream:

8. Make the whipped cream by adding the heavy cream and powdered sugar to a large bowl. Whip with a hand mixer to stiff peaks, about 7 minutes.

To decorate:

9. Spread the whipped cream over the entire surface of the cake, reserving about 1 cup of the whipped cream in a bowl.

10. Transfer the reserved whipped cream to a large piping bag. Trim off the tip of the piping bag to leave a 1-inch opening. Pipe piles of whipped cream to mimic the fluff on top of Whimsicott's head and its beard on the upper and lower edges of the top of the cake.

11. Transfer the curd to a pastry bag fitted with a large round tip. Pipe on two large curls around the hole in the center of the cake in the shape of Whimsicott's horns.

Kalos Region

Chespin Raspberry
Pistachio Napoleon

Dedenne Mango-Ginger
Bread Pudding

Pyroar Spicy
Pumpkin Empanadas

Tyrunt Chocolate
Crinkle Cookies

Floette Focaccia

Chespin
Raspberry Pistachio Napoleon

Puff pastry is normally baked up to be light golden brown, soft, crisp, and, well, puffy! To use puff pastry as the layers for a Napoleon, you bake it a special way so that it ends up denser and darker brown (but still flaky)— similar to how Chespin's soft quills can be flexed to become sharp and hard enough to pierce rock! The earthy brown pastry and pistachio cream reflect Chespin's colors, and these bright flavors, inspired by this Spiny Nut Pokémon, are sure to please.

Difficulty: ● ● ○ ○
Prep time: 25 minutes
Bake time: 25 minutes
Chill time: 4 hours
Yield: Serves 6 to 8
Dietary notes: Vegetarian

Equipment: 2 half-sheet pans, pizza cutter, heavy oven-safe pan (such as cast iron), wire cooling rack, medium saucepan, fine mesh strainer, two piping bags (one with small star tip)

1 sheet frozen puff pastry, thawed

½ cup sugar

3½ tablespoons cornstarch

½ teaspoon kosher salt

1 cup whole milk

1 cup heavy cream

3 ounces pistachio paste

2 tablespoons unsalted butter

4 to 6 drops green food coloring

Fresh raspberries

Powdered sugar

note: If you can't find pistachio paste, you can make it! Bring a pot of water to a boil, then add 1 cup of raw, shelled, whole pistachios and remove the pot from the heat. Let it sit for 1 to 2 minutes, then drain. Pour the pistachios onto a clean kitchen towel and lightly rub them to gently peel off the skins. If any skins are stuck, remove them gently with your fingers.

In a food processor, add the cleaned pistachios and process for 2 to 4 minutes, until pasty. Add water (about ¼ cup) and continue to process until smooth. This will make more than enough paste for this recipe—the rest can be stored in an airtight container for up to a week or frozen for up to 3 months.

1. Preheat the oven to 400°F. Line a half-sheet pan with parchment paper.

2. Use a pizza cutter or very sharp knife to cut the puff pastry into three equal rectangles. Place the pastry on the prepared sheet tray, then place another sheet of parchment on top of the pastry. Place the second sheet tray on top of the parchment-lined pastry, then weigh down the sheet pan with a heavy oven-safe pan (a cast-iron pan works great here!).

3. Bake the pastry for 20 minutes. Remove the pan, the second sheet tray, and the top layer of parchment. If the pastry is deep golden brown all over, it's ready to go. If not, bake for an additional 5 minutes until uniformly browned. Let the pastry cool completely on a wire rack.

4. Whisk together the sugar, cornstarch, and salt in a medium saucepan. Whisk in the milk and cream until smooth. Warm over medium heat until the mixture begins to thicken and bubble, stirring constantly with a rubber spatula to keep it from scorching.

5. Place the pistachio paste and butter into a medium bowl. Set a fine mesh strainer over the top of the bowl, and pour the milk mixture through the strainer. Stir the pistachio cream until smooth. If using, add the green food coloring and stir until homogenous.

6. Cover the pistachio cream with plastic wrap, pressing the plastic directly onto the surface of the cream (this prevents a skin from forming on top) and chill for 4 hours. After chilling, stir the cream until smooth, then scoop it into a piping bag fitted with a small star tip.

7. Lay one piece of the puff pastry on a platter. Alternate piping raspberry-sized rosettes of pistachio cream and placing raspberries on the puff pastry until it's completely covered. Carefully place a second piece of puff pastry on top. Repeat the alternating pattern of pistachio cream and raspberries until completely covered, reserving some of the pistachio cream. Top with the remaining piece of puff pastry.

8. Place a stiff card or piece of cardboard over part of the top of the pastry. Dust the top of the puff pastry with powdered sugar, leaving the covered section free of sugar. Transfer any remaining pistachio cream to a piping bag. Trim the tip of the piping bag to leave a ¼-inch opening. Pipe long quills clustered together on the sugar-free portion of the puff pastry in the pattern of Chespin's quills on top of its head. Keep chilled and serve cold.

Dedenne
Mango-Ginger Bread Pudding

The big chocolate whiskers that decorate this bread pudding aren't capable of sending electrical signals like Dedenne's whiskers. However, the mango nectar that goes into the custard base, along with the chunks of fresh mango throughout, give this pleasant dessert a bit of tang to zap your tongue, a perfect balance of sweet and tart for this Electric- and Fairy-type Pokémon. Dedenne emit electrical waves from their whiskers to communicate, but you'll need only one word when you're done with this dessert: Delicious.

Difficulty: ●○○○
Prep time: 15 minutes
Bake time: 45 minutes
Chill time: 4 hours
Yield: Serves 12
Dietary notes: Vegetarian

Equipment: 9-by-13-inch baking dish, wire cooling racks, half-sheet pan, microwave, piping bag with small round tip

1 cup whole milk

1 cup mango nectar

½ cup heavy cream

4 large eggs

¼ cup sugar

2 teaspoons ground ginger

1 tablespoon vanilla extract

18 ounces chopped mango

24 ounces stale brioche, cubed

½ cup chopped candied ginger

Dark chocolate

Dried papaya, cut into 2-inch rounds

1. Preheat the oven to 350°F. Grease a 9-by-13-inch baking dish.

2. Whisk together the milk, mango nectar, heavy cream, eggs, sugar, ground ginger, and vanilla in a very large bowl until smooth. Add the mango, brioche, and candied ginger, then gently fold and stir with a rubber spatula until evenly distributed and coated.

3. Pour the bread pudding mixture into the prepared baking dish. Bake for 45 minutes, until puffed, set, and light golden brown on top. Let cool completely on a wire rack, then cover and transfer to the fridge to chill for 4 hours.

4. Line a half-sheet pan with parchment. When the bread pudding is cooled, add the dark chocolate to a microwave-safe bowl. Heat the chocolate in the microwave in 30-second bursts, stirring each time, until it's melted and smooth. Transfer the chocolate to a piping bag fitted with a small round tip.

5. Pipe a large pair of Dedenne's whiskers onto the parchment. Chill in the freezer until completely set, about 5 minutes. While the chocolate chills, place the two papaya rounds onto the bread pudding to create Dedenne's cheek spots. Carefully remove the whiskers from the parchment and transfer onto the cooled bread pudding, placing the inner corners of the whiskers on the centers of the cheek spots.

Pyroar
Spicy Pumpkin Empanadas

Bite into one of these savory empanadas and you'll see bursts of color. Red from the bell peppers, orange from the pumpkin, and black from the black beans, all to match the colors on Pyroar's coat and mane. There's also a burst of heat from flavorful Fresno chiles, and the smokiness from paprika and cumin makes these taste like they were baked over a Pyroar's flames.

Difficulty: ● ● ○ ○
Prep time: 30 minutes
Chill time: 1 hour
Bake time: 20 minutes
Yield: 12 empanadas
Dietary notes: Vegetarian

Equipment: Food processor, large frying pan or cast-iron skillet, half-sheet pan

Dough

2 cups all-purpose flour

½ teaspoon kosher salt

8 tablespoons cold, unsalted butter, cubed

1 large egg

¼ cup very cold water

Filling

1 tablespoon olive oil

½ medium onion, peeled and finely chopped

½ red bell pepper, diced

1 teaspoon kosher salt

½ teaspoon black pepper

2 cloves garlic, minced

½ Fresno chile, deseeded and minced

½ teaspoon ground cumin

½ teaspoon smoked paprika

¼ teaspoon Mexican oregano

⅓ cup canned black beans, drained and rinsed

½ cup pumpkin purée

¼ cup shredded Monterey Jack cheese

1 large egg

1. Add the flour, salt, and butter to the bowl of a food processor. Pulse until the mixture resembles wet sand. Add the egg and cold water, and pulse to form a smooth dough. Shape the dough into a disc, wrap tightly with plastic, and chill for 1 hour.

2. Make the filling while the dough chills. Heat the oil in a large frying pan or cast-iron skillet over medium-high heat until shimmering. Add the onions and bell pepper, and season with the salt and pepper. Cook, stirring frequently, until softened and beginning to brown around the edges, about 5 minutes. Add the garlic, chile, cumin, paprika, and oregano, and continue to cook until fragrant, about 30 seconds. Add the beans and pumpkin purée, stirring to combine. Remove from heat. Taste and add more salt and pepper, if needed. Set aside.

3. Preheat the oven to 400°F. Line a half-sheet tray with parchment paper.

4. Place the chilled dough onto a floured work surface. Roll to a thickness of about ⅛ inch. Cut out six 6-inch circles using a small plate and sharp knife. Reroll the scraps and cut out more circles, repeating the process until you have 12 rounds.

5. Stir the shredded cheese into the filling. Beat the egg together with 1 tablespoon water. Scoop a small amount of filling into the center of each round. Brush the edges of each round with the egg wash. Fold the rounds in half over the filling.

6. Crimp the edges of the empanadas to seal them. If you're not confident with your crimping abilities, don't worry: Use the tines of a fork to press and seal the edges. Place the filled empanadas on the prepared sheet pan and brush the tops with the remaining egg wash.

7. Bake for 20 minutes, until the empanadas are golden brown. Let cool for 10 minutes, then serve hot; alternatively, transfer to a wire rack to cool completely and serve at room temperature.

Tyrunt
Chocolate Crinkle Cookies

Crinkle cookies are kind of magical because they go into the oven as powdered sugar–covered spheres, but they come out crinkled and craggy, sort of like the rocky hide on Tyrunt. Unlike a rock, though, these cookies are tender and chewy. Tyrunt love being pampered and hate sharing, but don't let them eat all your cookies!

Difficulty: ● ○ ○ ○
Prep time: 20 minutes
Chill time: 3 hours
Bake time: 26 minutes
Yield: About 18 cookies
Dietary notes: Vegetarian

Equipment: Stand mixer, hand mixer, piping bag, half-sheet pan, 2-tablespoon cookie scoop, wire cooling rack

Cookies

1 cup all-purpose flour
1 cup cocoa powder, divided
1 teaspoon baking soda
½ teaspoon kosher salt
8 tablespoons unsalted butter
½ cup sugar
½ cup packed light brown sugar
1 egg
1 cup powdered sugar

Frosting

1 cup powdered sugar
1 tablespoon orange zest
¼ teaspoon kosher salt
2 tablespoons unsalted butter, softened
¼ teaspoon vanilla extract
1 tablespoon orange juice

1. Whisk together the flour, ¾ cup cocoa powder, baking soda, and salt in a small bowl. Set aside.

2. Add the butter, sugar, and light brown sugar to the bowl of a stand mixer fitted with a paddle attachment. Beat on medium speed until light and fluffy, about 5 to 7 minutes. Add the egg, and beat until incorporated, about 2 minutes.

3. Reduce the mixer speed to low and add the flour mixture. Continue beating on low until combined into a soft, sticky dough. Cover the bowl and chill the dough in the fridge for 3 hours.

4. While the dough chills, make the orange frosting. Add the powdered sugar, orange zest, salt, butter, and vanilla to a medium bowl. Beat with a hand mixer on low until smooth. Add the orange juice 1 teaspoon at a time, beating between each addition, until the frosting is smooth but still quite thick. Transfer the frosting to a piping bag, seal, and set aside.

5. Toward the end of the dough chilling time, preheat the oven to 350°F. Line a half-sheet pan with parchment paper. Whisk the remaining ¼ cup cocoa powder with the powdered sugar in a small bowl until combined.

6. Scoop 9 portions of cookie dough with a 2-tablespoon cookie scoop from the bowl. If you don't have a cookie scoop, measure out 2 tablespoons of mix to create a portion. Cover and chill the remaining dough. Roll each portion into a ball, then roll in the cocoa and powdered sugar mixture until thickly coated. Place the balls on the prepared cookie sheet, leaving plenty of space between each cookie.

7. Bake the cookies for 10 to 13 minutes, until they have spread, puffed, and set. If the cookies don't look craggy, give the pan a sharp tap on the countertop to deflate them and create their signature craggy appearance. Let the cookies cool for 5 minutes before transferring them to a wire rack to cool completely.

8. Repeat steps 6 and 7 with the remaining cookie dough. Trim off the tip of the piping bag so there is about a ¼-inch opening. Pipe two large orange horns onto each cookie.

Floette
Focaccia

Plain focaccia is plenty delicious on its own, but you can use brightly colored toppings, such as mini bell peppers, grape tomatoes, olives, and fresh herbs, to turn your focaccia into a tasty work of art. In this recipe, we arrange herbs and veggies to look like a flower garden that even the most discerning Floette would love to inhabit.

Difficulty: ● ● ● ○
Prep time: 35 minutes
Rest time: 5 hours
Bake time: 25 minutes
Dietary notes: Nondairy, vegetarian

Equipment: Half-sheet pan

2½ cups lukewarm water

1 tablespoon honey

1 teaspoon active dry yeast

6 cups all-purpose flour

⅓ cup olive oil, plus more for pan and drizzling

Fresh herbs, such as rosemary, thyme, and chives

Red, yellow, and orange cherry tomatoes

Mini bell peppers

Olives

1. Whisk together the water, honey, and yeast in a large bowl. Let sit at room temperature until foamy, about 5 to 10 minutes. (If the mixture doesn't foam, the milk may be too warm. The ideal temperature should be between 100°F and 110°F. If it still doesn't foam, it's possible your yeast is dead, and you'll need to purchase new yeast.)

2. Add the flour and olive oil, then stir with a stiff rubber spatula or wooden spoon until no dry flour remains and a shaggy dough forms (the dough will be lumpy, with no dry flour remaining). Cover the bowl and let the dough sit at room temperature for 3 hours.

3. Pour enough olive oil in a half-sheet tray to coat the bottom with a thin layer (about 3 to 4 tablespoons). Tilt the pan each way until the olive oil completely coats the bottom. Slide your hand under the top edge of the dough, and fold the dough in on itself. Turn the bowl, and fold again, repeating the process 4 to 6 times.

4. Pour the dough into the prepared sheet pan. Flip over the dough to coat both sides, and then spread the dough to the edges as far as you can. (Don't worry if the dough doesn't fill the pan all the way.) Drizzle more olive oil (1 to 2 tablespoons, or to taste) on top of the dough, then cover it with plastic wrap. Let the dough rise for 2 more hours, until it is puffed and doubled in size.

5. Carefully stretch the dough to the edges of the pan, if needed, taking care not to deflate the dough too much.

6. Remove the tough, woody stems from the fresh herbs, leaving only tender stems and leaves. Cut some of the mini bell peppers crosswise to create small flowers, and cut some lengthwise into long spears to create petals for larger flowers.

7. Lay long chives along the long way of the pan to create stems. For longer stems, you can insert the fine points of some chives into the open end of other chives. Arrange the olives and cut peppers at the tips of the chives to create buds, small flowers, and large flowers. Place cherry tomatoes along either side of the chives to create flowers. Arrange the remaining fresh herbs along the bottom of the flower garden, and along the chive stems, to create green bushes, grass, and leaves for the flowers.

8. Bake the focaccia for 20 to 25 minutes, until golden brown. Drizzle with additional olive oil (2 to 3 tablespoons, or to taste). Let cool for 10 to 15 minutes before cutting and serving warm.

Alola Region

Pyukumuku Chocolate Roulade with Raspberry Whipped Cream

Mudbray Mud Pie

Comfey Tropical Pavlova

Mimikyu Chocolate Cupcakes with Praline Buttercream

Yungoos Toasted Coconut Chocolate Friands

Pyukumuku
Chocolate Roulade with Raspberry Whipped Cream

Pyukumuku are full of surprises, such as the slime they're coated in that keeps them moist. This roulade is full of surprises, too, with a rich chocolate cake and a tangy raspberry filling that'll smack your tastebuds and make you smile. To top it all off, this cake is also coated—but not with slime! This sweet, pink, raspberry-flavored whipped cream echoes the spikes on Pyukumuku's body and is a dazzling decoration, accompanied by a little whipped cream tail.

Difficulty: ● ● ● ○
Prep time: 30 minutes
Bake time: 25 minutes
Yield: Serves 8 to 10
Dietary notes: Gluten-free, vegetarian

Equipment: 9-by-13-inch metal baking pan, microwave, hand mixer, wire cooling rack, piping bag with large round tip

6 ounces dark chocolate

6 large eggs, separated

½ cup sugar

½ teaspoon salt

¼ cup cocoa powder, sifted

2 cups heavy cream

¼ cup powdered sugar

2 tablespoons raspberry powder

1. Preheat the oven to 350°F. Grease a 9-by-13-inch metal baking pan, then line it with parchment paper so that there is a 2-inch overhang on both short ends.

2. Add the dark chocolate to a microwave-safe bowl. Heat in 30-second bursts, stirring each time, until the chocolate is melted and smooth. Set aside to cool slightly.

3. Using a hand mixer, beat 6 egg yolks with the sugar and salt in a medium bowl until the mixture is thickened and light in color and the beaters leave ribbons behind them. With the beaters still going, slowly pour in the melted chocolate, beating until fully incorporated. Set aside.

4. Beat 6 egg whites in a large bowl with clean beaters (you can also do this in the bowl of a stand mixer fitted with a whisk attachment) until firm peaks form. Using a rubber spatula, carefully fold the egg whites into the chocolate mixture, about ⅓ at a time, until fully incorporated.

5. Sift the cocoa powder over the cake batter, and carefully fold it in with a rubber spatula until fully incorporated. Gently pour the batter into the prepared pan, gently spreading it evenly with the rubber spatula.

6. Bake for 25 minutes, until puffed and set. Lift the cake out of the pan and onto a wire rack. While the cake is still hot, carefully and gently roll it the long way into a tight roll, leaving the parchment on the cake. Let cool completely.

7. While the cake cools, make the whipped cream. Beat together the heavy cream and powdered sugar until medium peaks form. Reserve about ½ cup of the whipped cream in a small bowl, cover, and chill. Add the raspberry powder to the remaining whipped cream and continue beating to stiff peaks. Cover and chill until the cake is ready to fill.

8. Transfer the raspberry whipped cream to a piping bag fitted with a large round tip. Carefully unroll the cake while gently peeling off the parchment paper. Pipe a thin, even layer of the whipped cream on the unrolled cake, spreading with an offset spatula, if necessary. Reroll the cake and transfer it to a platter.

9. Pipe any remaining raspberry whipped cream in tall spikes all over the surface of the cake. Spoon the remaining plain whipped cream on one end of the top of the cake in a three-lobed puff, similar to Pyukumuku's tail. Slice the cake and serve immediately.

Mudbray
Mud Pie

Mudbray are happiest when they're allowed to eat dirt, make mud, and play in the mire. Mud is certainly the inspiration for this pie, which hails from Mississippi—it's said that the original mud pie was meant to emulate the dried-out mud flats. This pie is a must for chocolate fans: A chocolate cookie crust, a rich brownie layer, and a thick layer of luscious chocolate pudding, topped with mounds of whipped cream. These layers together resemble the mud that Mudbray loves so dearly.

Difficulty: ● ● ○ ○
Prep time: 45 minutes
Bake time: 40 minutes
Chill time: 4 hours
Yield: Serves 12
Dietary notes: Vegetarian

Equipment: 8-inch springform pan, small saucepan, wire cooling rack, medium saucier, hand mixer

Crust
8 tablespoons unsalted butter, melted
2½ cups chocolate cookie crumbs
½ teaspoon kosher salt

Brownie Layer
8 tablespoons unsalted butter
4 ounces dark chocolate
3 large eggs
½ cup packed light brown sugar
¼ cup sugar
1 tablespoon vanilla extract
⅓ cup all-purpose flour
½ teaspoon kosher salt
¼ cup cocoa powder, sifted
1 cup chopped pecans, toasted

To make the crust:

1. Preheat the oven to 350°F. Grease an 8-inch springform pan, then line the bottom with a circle of parchment paper.

2. Stir together the butter, cookie crumbs, and salt in a medium bowl until combined. Press the cookie crumbs into the bottom and completely up the sides of the pan. Use the flat bottom of a drinking glass or measuring cup to fully press the crust into the pan. Bake for 10 minutes. Set aside to cool while you make the brownie layer.

To make the brownie layer:

3. Add the butter and chocolate to a small saucepan, and melt over low heat, stirring constantly, until smooth and incorporated. Set aside to cool.

4. Using a hand mixer, beat the eggs together with the brown sugar, sugar, and vanilla in a large bowl until thickened and lighter in color, about 5 minutes. While continuing to beat, slowly add the melted chocolate and butter mixture, beating until incorporated.

5. Reduce the mixer speed to low and add the flour, salt, and cocoa, beating until just incorporated. Fold in the toasted pecans with a rubber spatula, then scrape the batter into the prepared crust. Bake for 25 to 30 minutes until just set and still slightly wobbly in the very center. Let the brownie cool completely in the pan on a wire rack.

note: Sauciers have a curved bottom, which makes them preferable when a mixture will likely get trapped in the edges of a straight-sided saucepan. A saucepan is okay to use if you don't have a saucier, but you'll have to be extra vigilant and thorough with stirring so that the mixture doesn't get trapped in the edges and burn.

continued on the next page

Pudding Layer

¾ cup whole milk

¾ cup heavy cream

2 tablespoons cornstarch

⅔ cup packed light brown sugar

¼ teaspoon kosher salt

3 large egg yolks

4 ounces dark chocolate

2 tablespoons unsalted butter

Whipped Cream Layer

2 cups heavy cream

¼ cup powdered sugar

Dark chocolate

To make the pudding layer:

6. Heat the milk and cream together in a medium saucier over medium heat until just beginning to steam. Whisk together the cornstarch, brown sugar, salt, and egg yolks in a medium bowl until smooth.

7. While whisking continuously, very slowly stream the hot milk and cream into the egg yolk mixture. When all the milk and cream has been added, transfer the mixture back to the saucier. Cook over medium heat, whisking gently but constantly, until the mixture begins to bubble. Once you see the first bubble, set a 1-minute timer and continue to whisk. Once the time is up, remove from heat.

8. Add the dark chocolate and butter to a medium bowl. Strain the milk mixture into the bowl. Let sit for a few minutes to allow the chocolate to melt, then stir until smooth. Cover with plastic wrap, pushing the plastic directly onto the surface of the pudding, and chill in the fridge for 4 hours.

To make the whipped cream:

9. Using a hand mixer, beat the heavy cream and powdered sugar in a large bowl until medium peaks form. Set aside.

To assemble:

10. Stir the pudding until smooth, then pour it over the brownie layer, smoothing the top with a spatula. Top with the whipped cream, and smooth with a spatula. Grate a piece of dark chocolate all over the top. Keep covered and chilled and serve cold.

Comfey
Tropical Pavlova

Pavlovas are a versatile dessert that can be topped with whatever seasonal fruit is available. We decorate this pavlova with lots of fresh tropical fruit in a pattern that makes it look like a giant flower that any Comfey would be proud to use to adorn its vine.

Difficulty: ● ○ ○ ○
Prep time: 15 minutes
Bake time: 1 hour
Rest time: 1 hour
Yield: Serves 8 to 12
Dietary notes: Gluten-free, vegetarian

Equipment: Half-sheet pan, stand mixer, piping bag, wire cooling rack, hand mixer

4 large egg whites

¼ teaspoon cream of tartar

1 cup sugar

½ teaspoon vanilla extract

1 cup heavy cream

1 tablespoon powdered sugar

Strawberries, sliced

Pineapple, cut and sliced into thin wedges

Kiwis, peeled, quartered, and thinly sliced

Mango, peeled, pitted, and sliced into thin wedges

note: No matter what you use, it's important to use fresh fruit in a pavlova. Frozen fruit releases too many juices as it thaws that seep into the meringue layer and make it soggy.

1. Preheat the oven to 300°F. Line a half-sheet pan with parchment paper.

2. Beat together the egg whites and cream of tartar in a stand mixer fitted with a whisk attachment until frothy. Increase the speed to medium-high, then slowly add the sugar. Continue whipping the egg whites until stiff peaks form. Add the vanilla and whip to combine.

3. Transfer the meringue to a piping bag. Trim off the tip to leave a 1-inch opening at the end. To keep the parchment from moving as you work, lift the corners of the parchment on the pan and smear a tiny dollop onto the pan at all four corners. Press the parchment down onto the meringue.

4. Pipe a 10-inch ring about 1½ inches high. Pipe smaller concentric circles that are about 1 inch high inside the 10-inch circle until it is completely filled in. If necessary, use an offset spatula to smooth the surface and fill in any gaps in the meringue.

5. Bake for 1 hour until set, but not browned. The meringue should look just off-white or cream-colored. Turn off the oven. Prop open the oven door with a wooden spoon, and let the meringue sit in the warm oven for an additional hour. Remove from oven and let cool completely on the pan set on a wire rack.

6. When the meringue base is completely cool, make the whipped cream. Using a handheld mixer, beat together the cream and the powdered sugar until soft peaks form, about 5 minutes. Spread the whipped cream in the center of the meringue, leaving the outermost ring bare.

7. Arrange the fruit in concentric circles, alternating colors for every circle, to make the pavlova look like a giant, multicolored flower. Serve immediately.

note: An extremely versatile dessert, pavlova can be made year-round with fresh, seasonal fruits—for example, with stone fruits, melons, and berries in the summer; with apples, figs, and stone fruits for an autumnal treat; with citrus fruits and cranberries in the winter; and with cherries, strawberries, and citrus in the spring. Winter citrus pavlovas, spring berry or passionfruit pavlovas, summer berry pavlovas, and autumnal apple or grape pavlovas are popular variations, but the only limit is your imagination.

Mimikyu
Chocolate Cupcakes with Praline Buttercream

Mimikyu wears a rag stitched together and decorated to look a bit like Pikachu, although that costume isn't fooling anyone. To contrast our bright, cheerful Pikachu cupcake (page 19), we created a Mimikyu cupcake that mirrors its visual appearance, but with a very different flavor profile. The result is a cupcake that's full of dark and mysterious flavors, with just a little crunch from the praline paste.

Difficulty: ● ● ● ○
Prep time: 45 minutes
Bake time: 18 minutes
Yield: 12 cupcakes
Dietary notes: Vegetarian

Equipment: 12-cup muffin tin, small saucepan, stand mixer, medium saucepan, hand mixer, four piping bags (one with large round tip), microwave, quarter-sheet pan

Cupcakes

2 ounces dark chocolate

½ cup buttermilk

½ cup coffee

½ cup cocoa powder

1 cup sugar

¼ cup neutral oil, such as canola or safflower

2 eggs, room temperature

1 tablespoon vanilla extract

¾ cup all-purpose flour

1 teaspoon kosher salt

½ teaspoon baking powder

½ teaspoon baking soda

Praline Buttercream

3 egg whites

¾ cup sugar

½ teaspoon kosher salt

¼ teaspoon cream of tartar

14 tablespoons unsalted butter, softened

¼ cup praline paste

To Assemble

White chocolate

Dark chocolate

Red candy melts

To make the cupcakes:

1. Preheat the oven to 350°F. Line a standard muffin tin with 12 paper cupcake liners (preferably brown paper to complement Mimikyu's colors, but whatever you have is fine!).

2. Add the dark chocolate, buttermilk, and coffee to a small saucepan. Cook, stirring constantly, over low heat until the chocolate is melted and the mixture is well combined. Stir in the cocoa powder until smooth, then remove from heat. Let cool slightly.

3. Add the sugar and oil to the bowl of a stand mixer fitted with a paddle attachment. Beat on low to combine, then add the eggs and vanilla, beating until smooth. With the mixer running, slowly add the buttermilk mixture. Increase the mixer speed to medium and beat until smooth and slightly thickened, about 5 minutes.

4. Reduce the mixer speed to low, and add the flour, salt, baking powder, and baking soda. Beat until just combined, then turn off the mixer. Scrape down the sides and bottom of the bowl with a rubber spatula to make sure the batter is homogenous.

5. Divide the batter between the liners and bake for 16 to 18 minutes, until a cake tester or toothpick inserted into the center of the cupcakes comes out clean. Let cool completely.

continued on the next page

To make the praline buttercream:

6. While the cupcakes cool, make the buttercream. Fill a medium saucepan with about ½ inch of water. Set over medium-low heat and allow it to come to a bare simmer. Add the egg whites, sugar, salt, and cream of tartar to a metal mixing bowl. Place the bowl on top of the saucepan, ensuring that the bowl isn't touching the water. Heat the mixture, whisking constantly, until the sugar is completely dissolved. Remove from heat.

7. Beat the egg white mixture with a handheld mixer on high until stiff peaks form and the mixture is room temperature, about 5 to 7 minutes. Add the softened butter, 2 tablespoons at a time, beating until fully incorporated before adding the next 2 tablespoons. The mixture may look soupy and curdled, but this is normal. Keep adding the butter and beating until the mixture is smooth and fluffy. Add the praline paste and beat to combine.

To assemble:

8. Transfer the buttercream to a piping bag fitted with a large round tip. Pipe a large, round dollop of buttercream on top of each cupcake until all the buttercream is used up. If the piping tip leaves any points on the frosting, wet your finger with cold water and smooth the frosting, wetting your finger every two cupcakes.

9. Add the white chocolate, dark chocolate, and red candy melts to separate microwave-safe bowls. Working one at a time, heat each bowl in 30-second bursts, stirring each time, until all three are melted and smooth. Add a very small amount of dark chocolate to the white chocolate and stir to make a tan color, adding more dark chocolate as needed to match the coloring of the buttercream. Transfer the two chocolates and candy melts to separate piping bags fitted with fine writing tips. (If you don't have enough tips, just snip off the very end of the piping bag tip to create a very small opening.)

10. Line a quarter-sheet pan with parchment paper. Pipe the white chocolate mixture into 12 spear shapes to create the base for Mimikyu's straight ear. Then pipe 12 spears that are bent in the middle to create the base of Mimikyu's lopsided ear.

11. Pipe a small amount of dark chocolate on the tips of all 24 ears to complete them. Chill the ears in the freezer until set (5 to 10 minutes), then carefully peel them off the parchment paper and insert them into the buttercream. Use the dark chocolate to pipe 2 messy spirals for Mimikyu's eyes directly onto each cupcake. Pipe a squiggly mouth on each cupcake with the dark chocolate.

12. Pipe 12 smaller messy scribbles beneath the eyes to create the red spots on Mimikyu's face.

Yungoos
Toasted Coconut Chocolate Friands

Yungoos will eat just about anything, especially because its stomach takes up most of its torso! But it's Yungoos's head that inspired these small, chewy almond cakes. These rich, filling friands would sate even the hungriest Yungoos's appetite, and the creamy color of the friand and chunks of chocolate match the brown coloring of its soft coat.

Difficulty: ● ○ ○ ○
Prep time: 10 minutes
Bake time: 25 minutes
Yield: 10 friands
Dietary notes: Vegetarian

Equipment: 12-cup muffin tin, wire cooling rack, microwave, 2 piping bags with small round tip and fine writing tip

8 tablespoons unsalted butter, melted and cooled

½ cup all-purpose flour

1 cup almond flour

1 cup toasted unsweetened coconut

5 large egg whites

½ cup sugar

½ teaspoon kosher salt

6 ounces dark chocolate, chopped

White chocolate

Dark chocolate

1. Preheat the oven to 350°F. Grease 10 cups in a standard muffin tin.

2. Stir together the butter, flour, almond flour, and toasted coconut in a medium bowl.

3. Whisk together the egg whites, sugar, and kosher salt in a small bowl until frothy. Stir the egg white mixture into the flour mixture. Fold in the chopped chocolate.

4. Divide the friand batter among the prepared cups. Bake for 20 to 25 minutes, until golden and set. Let the friands cool in the pan for 10 minutes, then transfer to a wire cooling rack to cool completely.

5. Add the white chocolate and dark chocolate to separate microwave-safe bowls. Heat the bowls in the microwave, separately, in 30 second bursts, stirring each time, until the chocolates are melted and smooth. Transfer the white chocolate to a piping bag fitted with a small round tip and transfer the dark chocolate to a piping bag fitted with a fine writing tip.

6. Use the white chocolate to pipe a long oblong mouth shape across the bottom of each cooled friand in the white chocolate, making sure to fill in the shape completely. Pipe an outline in dark chocolate around the oblong shape, then pipe a dark chocolate zigzag across the length of the shape to create Yungoos's teeth.

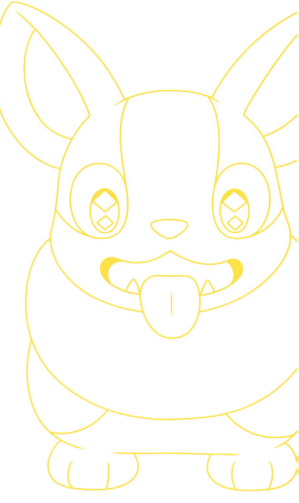

Galar Region

Dubwool Halva Brownies

Greedent Blueberry
Pecan Pie Bars

Yamper Mint Mocha Cake

Morpeko Double-Dipped
Viennese Cookies

Dubwool
Halva Brownies

Halva, a sweetened sesame candy, is normally quite dense and chewy, but when you crumble it up onto a hot brownie and bake for a minute or two in a hot oven, it melts and puffs up into a fluffy texture, just like Dubwool's coat. The nutty halva pairs beautifully with the dark chocolate brownie, creating a simple dessert that tastes complex, like it took much longer to make than it did. Dubwool's imposing horns are for impressing the opposite gender—imagine how many friends and guests you'll impress with this unique dessert!

Difficulty: ● ○ ○ ○
Prep time: 10 minutes
Bake time: 25 minutes
Yield: 16 brownies
Dietary notes: Vegetarian

Equipment: 8-by-8-inch baking pan, small saucepan, hand mixer

8 tablespoons unsalted butter
4 ounces dark chocolate
½ cup packed light brown sugar
¼ cup sugar
1 tablespoon vanilla
3 large eggs
⅓ cup all-purpose flour
¼ cup cocoa powder
½ teaspoon kosher salt
Plain halva
Chocolate halva

1. Preheat the oven to 350°F. Grease an 8-by-8-inch baking pan, then line it with parchment so that there's a 2-inch overhang on two sides.

2. Gently heat the butter and dark chocolate in a small saucepan over low heat until melted and smooth. Remove from heat and set aside to cool slightly.

3. Using a handheld mixer, beat the chocolate mixture with the brown sugar, sugar, and vanilla in a medium bowl until smooth, about 5 minutes. Add the eggs all at once and beat until the mixture is combined and smooth.

4. Reduce the mixer speed to low, and add the flour, cocoa, and salt, beating just to combine. Scrape the batter into the prepared pan and bake for about 23 minutes until just set—it will have a glossy top and be slightly wobbly in the center.

5. Crumble the plain halva all over the hot brownies. Crumble a smaller amount of the chocolate halva here and there over the plain halva. Return the pan to the oven until the halva is melted and slightly puffed, about 2 minutes more. Cool in the pan to room temperature.

6. Lift the cooled brownies out of the pan and transfer them to a cutting board. Cut into 16 brownies and serve.

Greedent
Blueberry Pecan Pie Bars

Greedent love to store berries in their tail. They particularly love Oran Berries, which resemble plump, juicy blueberries. We similarly hid a ton of blueberries in a tray of these pecan pie bars, and the result was a chewy, gooey, fruity filling on top of a crunchy crust. The toasty brown pecans are the cherry (or blueberry) on top, creating a nice crisp and a rich color reminiscent of Greedent's fluffy fur.

Difficulty: ● ● ○ ○
Prep time: 20 minutes
Bake time: 1 hour
Yield: 18 bars
Dietary notes: Vegetarian

Equipment: 9-by-13-inch baking dish, wire cooling rack

Crust
2 cups all-purpose flour
1 cup pecan flour
¼ cup packed light brown sugar
¾ teaspoon kosher salt
10 tablespoons unsalted butter, melted

Filling
4 eggs
½ cup honey
½ cup maple syrup
1 tablespoon vanilla extract
2 tablespoons cornstarch
1 teaspoon kosher salt
4 tablespoons unsalted butter, melted
12 ounces blueberries, fresh or frozen (no need to thaw)
1½ cups chopped pecans

1. Preheat the oven to 350°F. Grease a 9-by-13-inch baking dish. Line with parchment paper so there's a 2-inch overhang on the long sides of the dish.

2. Make the crust. Stir together the flour, pecan flour, brown sugar, and salt until combined. Stir in the butter until thoroughly mixed in. Press the crust into the bottom of the baking dish, using the flat bottom of a drinking glass or measuring cup to compress the crust. Bake for 12 minutes, until lightly golden and set.

3. Whisk together the eggs, honey, maple syrup, vanilla, cornstarch, salt, and butter until smooth. Fold in the blueberries and pecans until evenly dispersed. Pour it over the crust and bake until set, about 45 minutes.

4. Set the pan on a wire rack and let the pie cool completely. Loosen the edges with a thin knife, then lift the pie out of the baking dish. Transfer to a cutting board and cut into 18 bars.

Yamper
Mint Mocha Cake

Yamper is such a glutton for treats that it'll help its Trainer only in exchange for snacks. If you're trying to get your friends to help you with a big task, a surefire motivator is cake. This bright green, mint-flavored cake, its fluffy mocha buttercream, and the cute fondant details create the colors of Yamper's soft coat. Finish it off with a lightning bolt for this crackling Puppy Pokémon and you've got a masterpiece no one will turn down!

Difficulty: ● ● ○ ○
Prep Time: 45 minutes
Bake Time: 30 minutes
Yield: Serves 12 to 16
Dietary notes: Vegetarian

Equipment: Two 8-inch round cake pans, stand mixer, wire cooling rack, medium saucepan, hand mixer, offset spatula, two heart-shaped cookie cutters (one about 2½ inches long, one about 1¾ inches long)

Cake

1½ cups sugar

1 tablespoon baking powder

1 teaspoon kosher salt

12 tablespoons unsalted butter, softened

2 large eggs, room temperature

1 tablespoon vanilla extract

1½ teaspoons mint extract

3 to 5 drops green food coloring (optional)

2⅓ cups all-purpose flour

1⅓ cups whole milk, room temperature

Mocha Buttercream

3 egg whites

¾ cup sugar

½ teaspoon kosher salt

¼ teaspoon cream of tartar

14 tablespoons unsalted butter, softened

3 ounces dark chocolate, melted and cooled

1 teaspoon espresso powder mixed with 1 teaspoon hot water

Decorations

Pale green fondant

Pale yellow fondant

Powdered sugar, for dusting

To make the cake:

1. Preheat the oven to 350°F. Grease two 8-inch round cake pans, then line the bottoms with circles of parchment paper. Grease the parchment paper.

2. Add the sugar, baking powder, salt, and butter to the bowl of a stand mixer fitted with a paddle attachment. Mix on low until moistened, then increase the speed to medium-high and beat until light and fluffy, 5 to 7 minutes, scraping down the sides of the bowl with a rubber spatula about halfway through.

3. Add the eggs, one at a time, beating to incorporate fully before adding the next egg. Add the vanilla and mint extracts and the food coloring (if using), beating to combine.

4. Reduce the mixer speed to low, then add ⅓ of the flour and beat to combine. Pour in half the milk and beat until smooth. Repeat, adding ⅓ of the flour and the remaining milk; end with the last of the flour, beating just until incorporated, and scraping down the bowl and paddle with a rubber spatula as necessary.

5. Divide the batter between the two cake pans, spreading the batter evenly. Bake for 30 minutes, until a cake tester inserted into the center of the cakes comes out mostly clean, with just a few moist crumbs clinging to it. Let the cakes cool in the pans for about 10 minutes before turning them out onto a wire rack to cool completely.

To make the buttercream:

6. While the cakes cool, make the buttercream. Fill a medium saucepan with about ½ inch of water. Set over medium-low heat and allow the water to come to a bare simmer. Add the egg whites, sugar, salt, and cream of tartar to a metal mixing bowl. Place the bowl on top of the saucepan, ensuring that the bowl isn't touching the water. Heat the mixture, whisking constantly, until the sugar is completely dissolved. Remove from heat.

continued on the next page

7. Beat the egg white mixture with a handheld mixer on high until stiff peaks form and the mixture is room temperature, about 5 to 7 minutes. Add the softened butter, 2 tablespoons at a time, beating until fully incorporated, before adding the next 2 tablespoons. The mixture may look soupy and curdled, but this is normal. Keep adding the butter and beating until the mixture is smooth and fluffy.

8. Add the melted chocolate and espresso to the buttercream and beat to combine to make the mocha buttercream.

To decorate:

9. Place one of the cooled cakes on a platter. Spread about 1 cup of mocha buttercream on top, then place the second cake on top. Spread remaining mocha buttercream on the top and sides of the cake. Smooth the top and sides with an offset spatula.

10. Knead the pale green and pale yellow fondants separately on a clean, dry surface until smooth and pliable. Lightly dust the surface with powdered sugar and roll out the fondant (about $\frac{1}{10}$ inch thick). Using the larger heart-shaped cookie cutter (about 2½ inches in length), cut out 16 hearts out of the pale green fondant. Repeat with the pale yellow fondant, using a smaller heart-shaped cookie cutter (about 1¾ inches in length).

11. From the yellow fondant, cut out the lightning bolt in the shape of Yamper's tail (about 4 to 5 inches tall and 2 to 3 inches wide). Cut a long strip of yellow fondant to make the base decoration. Use a sharp knife or a pizza cutter to make the wavy top. Carefully press around the cake, trimming to fit and smoothing out the seam. Place the hearts evenly around the cake, pressing the yellow hearts in the center of the green hearts. Finish with the lightning bolt tail in the middle.

Morpeko
Double-Dipped Viennese Cookies

Morpeko can get irritable when it's hungry, which is almost always! Fortunately, these two-sided Viennese cookies are easy to scale up for double or even triple batches, enough to keep a Morpeko happily in Full-Belly Mode. To keep itself fed, Morpeko carries electrically roasted seeds, which it treasures—you'll consider these desserts your own precious treasure once you taste this tender, melt-in-your-mouth cookie. It's dipped in decadent dark chocolate to reflect this iconic Electric- and Dark-type Pokémon.

Difficulty: ● ○ ○ ○
Prep time: 15 minutes
Bake time: 15 minutes
Chill time: 30 minutes
Yield: 12 cookies
Dietary notes: Vegetarian

Equipment: Half-sheet pan, hand mixer, piping bag with large star tip, wire cooling rack, microwave

8 tablespoons unsalted butter, softened

¼ cup powdered sugar

¼ teaspoon kosher salt

1 teaspoon vanilla paste (or extract)

1 cup flour

2 tablespoons cornstarch

4 ounces dark chocolate

4 ounces milk chocolate

1. Preheat the oven to 375°F. Line a half-sheet pan with parchment paper.

2. Using a hand mixer, beat the butter, powdered sugar, salt, and vanilla paste on low speed in a medium bowl until moistened. Increase the speed to medium-high and beat until light and fluffy, about 5 to 7 minutes.

3. Sift together the flour and cornstarch over the butter mixture. Mix on low until moistened, then increase the speed to medium and mix until smooth and just incorporated. Transfer the dough to a piping bag fitted with a large star tip.

4. Pipe 12 large, closed figure eights onto the parchment paper, leaving about an inch between each one. Chill the entire sheet pan in the fridge for 30 minutes—this will help the cookies keep their shape while baking. If you're in a rush, you can freeze the dough for about 10 to 15 minutes.

5. Bake the cookies for 12 to 15 minutes until set and lightly golden. Let the cookies cool on the tray for 5 minutes, then transfer them to a wire rack to cool completely. Reserve the parchment-lined sheet tray.

6. Add the dark and milk chocolates to separate microwave-safe bowls. Microwave each bowl separately in 30-second bursts, stirring each time, until the chocolate is melted and smooth.

7. Grip a cookie in the center and dip one long side into the milk chocolate, allowing the excess to drip off before dipping the other side into the dark chocolate, leaving the middle of the cookie bare. Allow the excess dark chocolate to drip off the cookie, then set it on the reserved sheet pan to set. Repeat with the remaining cookies. Let the chocolate set, then serve.

PALDEA REGION

Sprigatito Pistachio Rose Rolls

Quaxly Blueberry Buckle

Fuecoco Spiced Ginger Loaf

Koraidon Mixed Berry Soufflé

Miraidon Lemon Cheesecake
& Ube Cake

Sprigatito
Pistachio Rose Rolls

Sprigatito gives off a scent that mesmerizes those around it. These rose-scented, pistachio-filled rolls have a similar effect, especially when you're icing the still-warm rolls. The edible rose petals scattered over the top, soft pink like Sprigatito's eyes, would make any Grass-type Pokémon happy. This recipe uses the tangzhong technique, which involves gelatinizing some of the flour before incorporating it into the dough. This improves the texture of the bread.

Difficulty: ● ● ● ○
Prep time: 30 minutes
Rest time: 2 hours
Bake time: 25 minutes
Yield: 12 rolls
Dietary notes: Vegetarian

Equipment: Small saucepan, stand mixer, 12-inch cast-iron pan, instant-read thermometer

Tangzhong

2 tablespoons all-purpose flour

¼ cup whole milk

Dough

4 cups all-purpose flour

1½ teaspoons kosher salt

2 teaspoons instant yeast

¼ cup packed brown sugar

1 cup whole milk

2 large eggs

4 tablespoons unsalted butter, softened

Filling

6 ounces pistachio paste

6 tablespoons unsalted butter, melted

¼ cup powdered sugar

2 tablespoons honey

1 tablespoon packed brown sugar

Icing

1½ cups powdered sugar

1 tablespoon orange juice

2 tablespoons heavy cream

½ teaspoon rose water

2 drops green food coloring (optional)

To Finish

Dried edible rose petals

Chopped pistachios

To make the tangzhong:

1. Whisk together the flour and milk in a small saucepan set over low heat. Cook until the mixture takes on a pudding-like consistency, about 3 minutes. Let cool.

To make the dough:

2. Add the flour, salt, yeast, and brown sugar to the bowl of a stand mixer fitted with a dough hook attachment. Mix on low to combine, then add the milk, both eggs, and the cooled tangzhong, mixing until a shaggy dough forms. Increase the mixer speed to medium-high and knead until smooth.

3. Add half the butter to the bowl and allow it to fully incorporate. Add the remaining butter. Continue kneading for 15 additional minutes, until the dough is smooth and elastic. Cover the dough and let it rise for about 1 hour, until puffed and doubled in size.

note: If you're unsure whether the dough is ready, tear off a small chunk. Stretch the dough—if you can stretch it enough to see through it without the dough tearing, it's ready to go. If the dough tears, continue mixing for 5 more minutes, then test it again. (This is called the windowpane test.)

To make the filling:

4. Meanwhile, make the filling by stirring together the pistachio paste and butter in a small bowl until smooth. Mix in the powdered sugar, honey, and brown sugar until smooth.

To assemble the rolls:

5. Preheat the oven to 350°F. Grease a 12-inch cast-iron pan.

6. When the dough has risen, gently punch it down to deflate, then turn it out onto a floured work surface. Roll the dough to a 20-by-12-inch rectangle. Spread the filling evenly over the surface of the dough, leaving a ½-inch border on both short edges and one long edge.

continued on the next page

7. Roll the dough into a tight coil, rolling toward the bare-bordered long edge. Pinch the seam to seal. Trim 1 inch off both ends to make an 18-inch-long log. Cut twelve 1½-inch-thick rounds and place them in the prepared pan, spacing them evenly. Cover the rounds and let them rise for about 1 hour, until they're puffed and crowding each other.

8. Bake the rolls for 25 minutes, until they're golden brown and an instant-read thermometer registers 195°F when inserted into the center of the rolls. Let cool slightly.

To make the icing and finish:

9. While the rolls cool, make the icing by combining the powdered sugar, orange juice, cream, rose water, and food coloring (if using) in a small bowl until smooth. Pour over the rolls while warm, spreading evenly. Scatter edible rose petals and chopped pistachios over the top and serve warm or at room temperature.

Quaxly
Blueberry Buckle

A buckle is a rich, dense cake (sort of like a coffee cake) packed with fruit, and this buckle is particularly fashionable! Quaxly uses cream as a styling product to keep the coif on its head slicked back, so we top each slice of this delicious blueberry buckle with coifs of blueberry-flavored whipped cream to honor this stylish Pokémon.

Difficulty: ●○○○
Prep time: 15 minutes
Bake time: 45 minutes
Yield: Serves 9
Dietary notes: Vegetarian

Equipment: 8-by-8-inch baking dish, hand mixer, wire cooling rack

Streusel Topping

½ cup packed light brown sugar

½ cup all-purpose flour

1 teaspoon cinnamon

¼ teaspoon nutmeg

¼ teaspoon kosher salt

4 tablespoons unsalted butter, melted

Buckle

2 cups all-purpose flour

2 teaspoons baking powder

½ teaspoon kosher salt

6 tablespoons unsalted butter, softened

½ cup sugar

2 eggs

½ cup sour cream

2 cups blueberries (fresh or frozen, no need to thaw)

Whipped Cream

1 cup heavy cream

1 tablespoon sugar

2 teaspoons blueberry powder, or 1 tablespoon blueberry juice

1. Preheat the oven to 375°F. Grease an 8-by-8-inch baking dish.

2. Make the streusel topping by stirring together all the ingredients in a small bowl until it resembles wet sand. Set aside.

3. Make the buckle. Whisk together the flour, baking powder, and salt in a small bowl.

4. Using a handheld mixer on medium, beat together the butter and sugar in a medium bowl for about 5 to 7 minutes, until light and fluffy. Beat in the eggs, mixing until smooth.

5. Reduce the mixer speed to low, and add half the flour mixture, mixing until just combined. Add the sour cream and mix until smooth, then add the remaining flour mixture. Mix until just incorporated. Gently fold the blueberries into the batter using a rubber spatula.

6. Pour the batter into the prepared pan and spread it evenly. Sprinkle the streusel topping all over the top. Bake for 45 minutes until golden brown and a cake tester inserted into the center of the buckle comes out clean (blueberry juice doesn't count!). Place the pan on a wire rack and let the buckle cool in the pan to room temperature.

7. Whip the heavy cream, sugar, and blueberry powder in a medium bowl until medium peaks form. Cut the blueberry buckle, and serve each slice with a tall dollop of blueberry whipped cream, sweeping some of the dollop in front to the right to emulate Quaxly's signature hairstyle. Store any leftover whipped cream and buckle separately: Keep the whipped cream covered and in the fridge, and keep the buckle covered at room temperature.

Fuecoco
Spiced Ginger Loaf

Fuecoco stores fire energy on the scales on its stomach, then releases it from the dent on top of its head. That energy flickers to and fro! This spicy ginger loaf is packed with so many delicious warming spices that some heat sticks out of the top (in the form of candied ginger), just like Fuecoco's leaking fire energy.

Difficulty: ● ○ ○ ○
Prep time: 15 minutes
Bake time: 40 minutes
Yield: Serves 8 to 12
Dietary notes: Vegetarian

Equipment: 9-by-5-inch loaf pan, stand mixer, instant-read thermometer, wire cooling rack

Loaf

8 tablespoons unsalted butter, softened
¼ cup honey or molasses
¾ cup packed light brown sugar
2 large eggs, room temperature
½ cup buttermilk, room temperature
1 tablespoon vanilla extract
2 cups all-purpose flour
2 teaspoons baking powder
1 teaspoon ground ginger
2 teaspoons cinnamon
¼ teaspoon ground clove
¼ teaspoon allspice
¼ teaspoon cayenne
¼ teaspoon nutmeg

Icing

1 cup powdered sugar
½ teaspoon cinnamon
2 tablespoons milk (any percentage)
4 to 6 drops red food coloring (optional)
Yellow food coloring (optional)

Decoration

Candied ginger, cut into 2 long strips

1. Preheat the oven to 350°F. Grease a 9-by-5-inch loaf pan.

2. In the bowl of a stand mixer fitted with a paddle attachment, beat together the butter, honey, and brown sugar on medium until light and fluffy. Mix in the eggs until fully incorporated, followed by the buttermilk and vanilla.

3. Reduce the mixer speed to low, and add the flour, baking powder, ginger, cinnamon, clove, allspice, cayenne, and nutmeg. Mix until combined.

4. Scrape the batter into the prepared pan, and bake for 40 minutes, until an instant-read thermometer inserted into the center of the loaf registers 195°F. Let the cake cool in the pan for 5 minutes before turning out onto a wire rack to cool completely.

5. For the icing, mix the powdered sugar, cinnamon, and milk together until smooth and thick. If using food coloring, divide the icing into thirds, separating each third into a clean bowl. Add 3 to 5 drops of red food coloring to one bowl to create red icing, 1 drop red food coloring and 3 to 5 drops yellow food coloring to the second bowl to create orange icing, and 4 to 6 drops yellow food coloring to the third bowl to create yellow icing. Stir each icing until uniform in color.

6. Pour over the top of the loaf in a flame shape, starting with the yellow icing, then accenting with orange and red icing to create flame patterns however you'd like, allowing the excess to drip down the sides of the loaf. If needed, shape the icing into the flame shape or feather through the colors with the sharp tip of a knife.

7. Poke one hole in the center of the loaf with a chopstick. Insert one long strip and one shorter strip of candied ginger into the hole to create the leaking fire energy on Fuecoco's head.

Koraidon
Mixed Berry Soufflé

Soufflés are notorious for being one of the most difficult desserts to make—a challenge befitting a Legendary Pokémon like Koraidon. You must be patient and leave the oven door closed for the entire baking process, or the delicate soufflé will sink. This soufflé is extra difficult to make because it requires two separate berry purées to be mixed into the base, and then gently combined and swirled before baking. Work quickly and carefully, and trust your training. The fruit purées used to flavor the soufflé are also drizzled on at the end, both to reinforce the strong berry flavors and to mirror Koraidon's vibrant coloring.

Difficulty: ● ● ● ●
Prep time: 30 minutes
Bake time: 30 minutes
Yield: Serves 4 to 6
Dietary notes: Gluten-free, nondairy, vegetarian

Equipment: 48-ounce soufflé dish, small saucepan, blender, hand mixer, butcher's twine, paperclip

4 ounces frozen blueberries

4 ounces frozen blackberries

6 ounces frozen strawberries

4 ounces frozen raspberries

4 large eggs, separated

½ cup sugar, plus 2 tablespoons sugar for the soufflé dish

2 teaspoons cornstarch

1 tablespoon lemon juice

¼ teaspoon kosher salt

note: A soufflé dish is a straight-sided, heat-proof baking dish made specifically for making soufflés. It's typically made from porcelain, and the straight, tall sides help soufflés achieve their signature rise.

1. Preheat the oven to 400°F. Butter the inside of a 48-ounce soufflé dish. Sprinkle 2 tablespoons sugar inside. Rotate the dish to evenly coat, then tap out the excess.

2. Add the blueberries and blackberries to a small saucepan. Cook on medium-low, stirring occasionally, until the berries break down and release their juices, about 5 to 7 minutes. Let cool.

3. Repeat step 2 with the strawberries and raspberries.

4. Add the blueberry mixture to a blender and blend on high until smooth. Strain, then measure ¼ cup of the purée into a small bowl; reserve the rest to serve. Rinse out the blender, and repeat the process with the strawberry mixture, keeping the berry purées separate. Set aside.

5. Using a handheld mixer on high, beat the egg yolks with the sugar in a medium bowl for about 8 minutes, until the yolks are thick and light and the beaters leave ribbons as you move them through the bowl.

6. Whisk together the cornstarch and lemon juice in a small bowl until smooth, then beat it into the egg yolk mixture, along with the salt. Divide this mixture into 2 medium bowls. Stir the blueberry/blackberry purée into one of the bowls, then stir the strawberry/raspberry purée into the other.

7. Whip the egg whites in a large bowl with a clean handheld mixer until stiff peaks form. (It is extremely important that the beaters be completely clean, or the egg whites won't whip to the correct consistency.)

8. Quickly and gently fold half the whipped egg whites into the blueberry mixture using a rubber spatula until just incorporated. Fold the remaining whipped egg whites into the strawberry mixture.

continued on the next page

9. Simultaneously pour both batters into the prepared soufflé dish. Using a butter knife, carefully swirl the two mixtures together (this will also knock out any large pockets of air in the batter, but be careful not to overdo it— six passes through the batter should be plenty).

10. Quickly spray a thin layer of cooking spray onto a sheet of parchment paper, then use the parchment to create a collar by wrapping it around the soufflé dish and securing it with butcher's twine. The collar should extend 4 inches past the top of the soufflé dish. Secure the overlapping seam at the top of the parchment with a paper clip.

11. Bake for 30 minutes, until the soufflé is puffed, risen, and lightly browned on top. Carefully remove the parchment collar and serve immediately, before the soufflé collapses. Drizzle each serving with the remaining berry purées.

Miraidon
Lemon Cheesecake & Ube Cake

It's time to prove your mettle as a Pokémon Train— . . . um, baker, and put your skills to the test. As with battling a Legendary Pokémon, this recipe requires you to use many precise skills and techniques. The luscious lemon cheesecake layer and frosting feel electric on your palate, and the cheesecake is even better sandwiched between two rich, delicately sweet layers of purple ube cake. You'll feel powerful when you make this epic dessert, which is worthy of the Iron Serpent!

Difficulty: ● ● ● ●
Prep time: 1½ hours
Bake time: 1 hour and 25 minutes
Chill time: 4 hours
Yield: Serves 12 to 16
Dietary notes: Vegetarian

Equipment: 8-inch springform pan, stand mixer, wire cooling rack, two 8-inch round cake pans, hand mixer, piping bag with small round tip

Cheesecake

Two 8-ounce packages cream cheese, softened

½ cup sour cream, room temperature

½ cup sugar

2 teaspoons vanilla extract

2 teaspoons lemon zest

2 large eggs, room temperature

2 tablespoons lemon juice

1 tablespoon all-purpose flour

1 tablespoon cornstarch

Ube Cakes

1½ cups sugar

1 cup neutral oil, such as canola or safflower

8 tablespoons unsalted butter, softened

2 large eggs

2 teaspoons vanilla extract

1 tablespoon ube extract

2½ cups cake flour

1½ teaspoons baking soda

1 teaspoon kosher salt

1 cup buttermilk

NOTE: Ube is a bright purple yam, and its flavor is similar to sweet potato. It pairs well with not only lemon, but also other sweets, such as vanilla, coconut, mango, guava, passionfruit, and even cheese!

To make the lemon cheesecake:

1. Preheat oven to 325°F. Grease an 8-inch springform pan, and line the bottom of the pan with a circle of parchment paper.

2. Beat the cream cheese, sour cream, sugar, vanilla, and lemon zest in the bowl of a stand mixer on medium-low until smooth. Beat in the eggs, one at a time, beating until fully incorporated before adding the next egg.

3. Whisk together the lemon juice with the flour and cornstarch in a small bowl until smooth. Beat into the cream cheese mixture until incorporated.

4. Pour the cheesecake batter into the prepared springform pan, smoothing the top with a rubber spatula. Bake for 45 to 55 minutes, until lightly golden and set, with just a slight wobble in the center. Turn off the oven, and prop open the door with a wooden spoon, allowing the cheesecake to slowly cool in the warm oven for 30 minutes before transferring the pan to a wire rack to cool completely. Cover and chill the pan for 4 hours.

To make the ube cakes:

5. Preheat the oven to 350°F. Grease two 8-inch cake pans, then line the bottoms with circles of parchment paper.

6. In the bowl of a stand mixer fitted with a paddle attachment, cream the sugar, oil, and butter together until smooth, about 5 minutes. Add the eggs one at a time, beating to incorporate before adding the next egg. Mix in the vanilla and ube extracts, beating until evenly colored.

7. Sift together the cake flour, baking soda, and salt into a small bowl. Add ⅓ of the flour mixture to the batter, mixing on low until just incorporated. Add half the buttermilk, mixing until smooth, then repeat the process with the remaining flour mixture and buttermilk, ending with the flour mixture.

8. Divide the batter between the prepared cake pans, spreading evenly. Bake for 30 minutes, until a cake tester inserted into the center of the cake comes out clean, with just a few moist crumbs clinging to it.

9. Let the cakes cool in the pans for 10 minutes before turning them out onto a wire rack to cool completely.

continued on the next page

Frosting

Two 8-ounce packages of cream cheese, softened

16 tablespoons unsalted butter, softened

2 teaspoons lemon zest

2 teaspoons vanilla extract

3 cups powdered sugar

2 tablespoons heavy cream, plus more if needed

6 drops yellow food coloring

1 to 3 drops ube extract (see note on page 135)

Silver sugar ball decorations

NOTE: If you'd like exceptionally clean lines when creating the tire track pattern, you can use pale purple and white fondant instead. Lay them over the yellow frosting, then press in the silver sugar balls as described.

To make the frosting:

10. Using a hand mixer on medium speed, beat together the cream cheese and butter in a large bowl until completely smooth. Mix in the lemon zest and vanilla until combined.

11. Reduce the mixer speed to low and add the powdered sugar 1 cup at a time, mixing until moistened. Add the heavy cream, increase the speed to medium-high, and mix until smooth, about 8 to 10 minutes. If the frosting is too thick, add more heavy cream as needed until it reaches a soft, spreadable consistency but still holds its shape.

12. Remove ½ cup of frosting and transfer to a separate bowl, then remove a second ½ cup of frosting and transfer to a separate bowl. Add 4 to 6 drops yellow food coloring to the largest amount of frosting, and beat until uniform in color. If needed, add more yellow food coloring to closer match Miraidon's coloring. Add 1 drop of ube extract to one of the bowls with ½ cup of reserved frosting. Stir to combine to make pale purple frosting. If needed, add an additional drop or two of ube extract to match Miraidon's light purple coloring. Leave the remaining ½ cup of reserved frosting uncolored.

To assemble:

13. If the ube cakes have domed, trim off the tops with a serrated knife so they are flat and level. (It is very important that the cakes are level; otherwise, the cake might fall over!)

14. Place one of the ube cakes on a platter. Spread ¾ cup of yellow frosting over the top of the cake. Use a paring knife to loosen the cheesecake from the sides of the springform pan. Release and remove the body of the springform pan, then place a plate on top of the cheesecake. Invert the cheesecake, peel off the parchment, then place the cheesecake on top of the frosted cake. Spread ¾ cup of yellow frosting over the top of the cheesecake. Add the final layer of cake and spread the remaining yellow frosting over the top and sides of the cake. Spread the light purple frosting in a thick line over the cake to create Miraidon's belly, extending down the cake sides.

15. Fill a piping bag with the reserved uncolored frosting fitted with a small round tip. Pipe the white tread marks on Miraidon's belly on the cake across the light purple frosting, and extending slightly over onto the yellow frosting. Carefully place 20 or so silver candy ball decorations all around the light purple part of the cake to mimic the sparkles on Miraidon's belly.

Measurement Conversions

VOLUME

US	Metric
⅛ teaspoon	1 ml
1 teaspoon	5 ml
1 tablespoon	15 ml
1 fluid ounce	30 ml
⅛ cup	50 ml
¼ cup	60 ml
⅓ cup	80 ml
3.4 fluid ounces	100 ml
½ cup	120 ml
⅔ cup	160 ml
¾ cup	180 ml
1 cup	240 ml
1 pint (2 cups)	480 ml
1 quart (4 cups)	.95 liter

TEMPERATURES

Fahrenheit	Celsius
200°	93.3°
212°	100°
250°	120°
275°	135°
300°	150°
325°	163°
350°	177°
400°	205°
425°	218°
450°	232°
475°	246°

WEIGHT

US	Metric
0.5 ounce	14 grams
1 ounce	28 grams
¼ pound	113 grams
⅓ pound	151 grams
½ pound	227 grams
1 pound	454 grams

Dietary Considerations

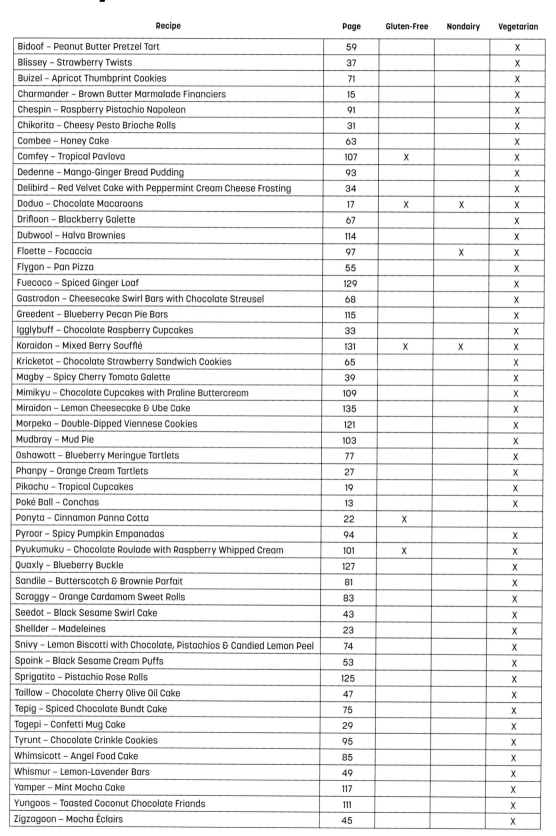

Recipe	Page	Gluten-Free	Nondairy	Vegetarian
Bidoof – Peanut Butter Pretzel Tart	59			X
Blissey – Strawberry Twists	37			X
Buizel – Apricot Thumbprint Cookies	71			X
Charmander – Brown Butter Marmalade Financiers	15			X
Chespin – Raspberry Pistachio Napoleon	91			X
Chikorita – Cheesy Pesto Brioche Rolls	31			X
Combee – Honey Cake	63			X
Comfey – Tropical Pavlova	107	X		X
Dedenne – Mango-Ginger Bread Pudding	93			X
Delibird – Red Velvet Cake with Peppermint Cream Cheese Frosting	34			X
Doduo – Chocolate Macaroons	17	X	X	X
Drifloon – Blackberry Galette	67			X
Dubwool – Halva Brownies	114			X
Floette – Focaccia	97		X	X
Flygon – Pan Pizza	55			X
Fuecoco – Spiced Ginger Loaf	129			X
Gastrodon – Cheesecake Swirl Bars with Chocolate Streusel	68			X
Greedent – Blueberry Pecan Pie Bars	115			X
Igglybuff – Chocolate Raspberry Cupcakes	33			X
Koraidon – Mixed Berry Soufflé	131	X	X	X
Kricketot – Chocolate Strawberry Sandwich Cookies	65			X
Magby – Spicy Cherry Tomato Galette	39			X
Mimikyu – Chocolate Cupcakes with Praline Buttercream	109			X
Miraidon – Lemon Cheesecake & Ube Cake	135			X
Morpeko – Double-Dipped Viennese Cookies	121			X
Mudbray – Mud Pie	103			X
Oshawott – Blueberry Meringue Tartlets	77			X
Phanpy – Orange Cream Tartlets	27			X
Pikachu – Tropical Cupcakes	19			X
Poké Ball – Conchas	13			X
Ponyta – Cinnamon Panna Cotta	22	X		
Pyroar – Spicy Pumpkin Empanadas	94			X
Pyukumuku – Chocolate Roulade with Raspberry Whipped Cream	101	X		X
Quaxly – Blueberry Buckle	127			X
Sandile – Butterscotch & Brownie Parfait	81			X
Scraggy – Orange Cardamom Sweet Rolls	83			X
Seedot – Black Sesame Swirl Cake	43			X
Shellder – Madeleines	23			X
Snivy – Lemon Biscotti with Chocolate, Pistachios & Candied Lemon Peel	74			X
Spoink – Black Sesame Cream Puffs	53			X
Sprigatito – Pistachio Rose Rolls	125			X
Taillow – Chocolate Cherry Olive Oil Cake	47			X
Tepig – Spiced Chocolate Bundt Cake	75			X
Togepi – Confetti Mug Cake	29			X
Tyrunt – Chocolate Crinkle Cookies	95			X
Whimsicott – Angel Food Cake	85			X
Whismur – Lemon-Lavender Bars	49			X
Yamper – Mint Mocha Cake	117			X
Yungoos – Toasted Coconut Chocolate Friands	111			X
Zigzagoon – Mocha Éclairs	45			X

Difficulty Index

About the Author

Jarrett Melendez grew up on the mean, deer-infested streets of Bucksport, Maine. A former chef and line cook, Jarrett has worked in restaurants, diners, and bakeries throughout New England and Mexico, and got instruction on Japanese home cooking from some very patient host mothers when he lived in Tokyo and Hiroshima. He's been a professional writer since 2009, but started working as a recipe developer and food writer in 2020. His work has appeared on *Bon Appétit*, *Saveur*, *Epicurious*, and *Food52*, and he is the author of *The Comic Kitchen*, an upcoming fully illustrated, comic-style cookbook. When not cooking and writing about food, Jarrett is also an award-winning comic book writer. His best known work is *Chef's Kiss* from Oni Press, which won the Alex Award from the American Library Association, along with a GLAAD award nomination for Outstanding Graphic Novel. Jarrett has contributed to the Ringo-nominated *All We Ever Wanted*, *Full Bleed*, *Young Men in Love*, and *Murder Hobo: Chaotic Neutral*. He is currently working on *Tales of the Fungo: The Legend of Cep*, a middle-grade fantasy adventure, to be published by Andrews McMeel. He lives in Massachusetts with his collection of Monokuro Boo plush pigs.

INSIGHT EDITIONS

PO Box 3088
San Rafael, CA 94912
www.insighteditions.com

Find us on Facebook: www.facebook.com/InsightEditions
Follow us on Instagram: @insighteditions

Published by Insight Editions, San Rafael, California, in 2024.
No part of this book may be reproduced in any form without written permission from the publisher.

Collection ISBN: 979-8-88663-822-6

Publisher: Raoul Goff
VP, Co-Publisher: Vanessa Lopez
VP, Creative: Chrissy Kwasnik
VP, Manufacturing: Alix Nicholaeff
VP, Group Managing Editor: Vicki Jaeger
Publishing Director: Mike Degler
Senior Designer: Judy Wiatrek Trum
Associate Editor: Sadie Lowry
Editorial Assistant: Alex Figueiredo
Managing Editor: Maria Spano
Senior Production Editor: Katie Rokakis
Production Associate: Deena Hashem
Senior Production Manager, Subsidiary Rights: Lina s Palma-Temena

Text by Jarrett Melendez
Photographer: Elysa Weitala
Food Stylist: Alexa Hyman
Assistant Food Stylist: Hirumi Shimizu
Assistant Food Stylist: Sybil Johnson
Photoshoot Art Direction: Judy Wiatrek Trum

ROOTS of PEACE   REPLANTED PAPER

Insight Editions, in association with Roots of Peace, will plant two trees for each tree used in the manufacturing of this book. Roots of Peace is an internationally renowned humanitarian organization dedicated to eradicating land mines worldwide and converting war-torn lands into productive farms.

Manufactured in China by Insight Editions
10 9 8 7 6 5 4 3 2 1